ASSURED PATHWAYS TO PROSPERITIES

BY

JEFF KENNEDY

TABLE OF CONTENTS

A- Introduction

B- The laws (1-55)

The Law of Differentiation
The Law of Cost-Benefit Analysis
The Law of Scalability
The Law of Adaptability
The Law of Decision Making
The Law of Teamwork
The Law of Delegation
The Law of Time Management
The Law of Integrity
The Law of Ethical Conduct
The Law of Transparency
The Law of Trust
The Law of Collaboration
The Law of Partnerships
The Law of Networking
The Law of Negotiation
The Law of Sales
The Law of Pricing
The Law of Revenue Generation
The Law of Profitability
The Law of Return on Investment (ROI)
The Law of Cash Conversion Cycle
The Law of Break-even Analysis
The Law of Financial Management
The Law of Budgeting
The Law of Capital Investment
The Law of Debt Management
The Law of Risk Management
The Law of Crisis Management
The Law of Customer Relationship Management (CRM)
The Law of Customer Retention
The Law of Customer Loyalty
The Law of Market Segmentation
The Law of Targeting
The Law of Customer Acquisition

A

INTRODUCTION

In the ever-changing landscape of the business world, entrepreneurs and professionals must recognize the existence of certain fundamental laws that govern the dynamics of success. These laws, though intangible, shape the outcomes of ventures, influence decision-making, and impact long-term sustainability. By understanding and embracing these inevitable laws, businesses can position themselves for growth and navigate the challenges they face. This article delves into five key laws that are inherently tied to the fabric of business, shedding light on their significance and offering insights on how to leverage them to thrive in a competitive environment.

At the core of every successful business lies the ability to create value for its customers. The Law of Value Creation emphasizes that sustainable success can only be achieved by meeting the needs and desires of target markets. Businesses that prioritize customer-centricity, innovation, and quality in their products or services are more likely to establish a loyal customer base, gain a competitive edge, and drive growth. By focusing on value creation, businesses can foster long-term relationships, build brand equity, and adapt to ever-evolving customer preferences.

Change is the only constant in the business world. The Law of Adaptability underscores the necessity for businesses to be flexible and responsive to external and internal shifts. Organizations that embrace change, anticipate market trends and readily adapt their strategies, products, and operations are better equipped to thrive amidst disruption. Being adaptable empowers businesses to seize opportunities, mitigate risks, and maintain relevance in an ever-evolving marketplace.

In a highly interconnected and interdependent world, the Law of Collaboration highlights the importance of partnerships and alliances. No business exists in isolation, and successful organizations recognize the power of collaboration. Through strategic collaborations, businesses can leverage complementary strengths, access new markets, share resources, and foster innovation. Collaboration enables companies to achieve collective growth, expand their reach, and enhance their competitive advantage.

Effective leadership lies at the heart of every prosperous business. The Law of Leadership underscores the significance of visionary leaders who inspire, motivate, and guide their teams toward achieving shared goals. Strong leadership cultivates a positive work culture, encourages employee engagement, and drives innovation and productivity. By investing in leadership development and nurturing a culture of continuous learning, businesses can unlock the full potential of their workforce and foster sustainable growth.

Integrity and ethical conduct form the bedrock of enduring success. The Law of Ethics and Integrity emphasizes that businesses must operate with honesty, transparency, and ethical principles. Organizations that prioritize integrity in their decision-making, relationships with stakeholders, and social responsibility create trust and credibility. Upholding ethical standards not only enhances the reputation and brand value of a business but also ensures long-term sustainability and mitigates the risk of legal and reputational damage.

The inevitable laws of business shape the trajectory of enterprises, dictating their success or failure. By recognizing and adhering to these laws, businesses can position themselves for growth, adapt to change, foster collaboration, inspire leadership, and uphold ethical standards. The journey toward sustainable success in the business world requires constant evaluation, evolution, and innovation. By embracing these laws and incorporating them into their strategies and operations, businesses can navigate challenges, seize opportunities, and build a solid foundation for long-term prosperity.

While there isn't a universally agreed-upon list of " laws of business," there are fundamental laws and concepts that are commonly recognized in the business world. In the next chapter of this book, we shall be examining the 55 key principles that encompass various aspects of business.

B

THE LAWS(1-55)

1

The Law of Supply and Demand
The law of supply and demand is an economic principle that explains the relationship between the availability of a product or service (supply) and the desire for that product or service (demand). It states that the price of a good or service in a market will settle at a point where the quantity supplied by producers equals the quantity demanded by consumers.

According to the law of supply, as the price of a product increases, the quantity supplied by producers also increases, assuming other factors remain constant. This is because higher prices incentivize producers to increase their output and profit from the increased revenue.

On the other hand, according to the law of demand, as the price of a product increases, the quantity demanded by consumers decreases, assuming other factors remain constant. This is because higher prices reduce the purchasing power of consumers, making the product relatively more expensive and less attractive.

The interaction of supply and demand determines the equilibrium price and quantity in a market. When the quantity supplied exceeds the quantity demanded, there is a surplus, and producers may be motivated to lower prices to sell their excess inventory. Conversely, when the quantity demanded exceeds the quantity supplied, there is a shortage, and producers may increase prices to maximize profits.

The law of supply and demand is a fundamental concept in economics and plays a crucial role in determining prices, production levels, and market behavior. It helps explain how markets allocate resources and how changes in supply or demand can affect equilibrium prices and quantities.

2

The Pareto Principle (80/20 Rule)

The Pareto Principle, also known as the 80/20 rule, is a concept that states that roughly 80% of the effects come from 20% of the causes or inputs. This principle is named after Italian economist Vilfredo Pareto, who observed in the early 20th century that approximately 80% of the land in Italy was owned by 20% of the population.

The Pareto Principle has since been applied to various fields and contexts beyond economics. It suggests that in many situations, a small number of factors or inputs have a disproportionately large impact or account for the majority of the results or outcomes. Conversely, a large number of factors have a relatively small impact or account for a minority of the results.

For example, in business, it is often observed that roughly 80% of a company's sales come from 20% of its customers. Similarly, 80% of a company's problems may stem from 20% of its processes or employees. In personal productivity, the Pareto Principle suggests that 80% of your results come from 20% of your efforts or activities.

It's important to note that the 80/20 split is not always exact. It can vary, such as 90/10 or 70/30, but the general principle remains the same: a small portion of inputs or causes drive a large portion of the outputs or results.

Understanding the Pareto Principle can be valuable in decision-making, resource allocation, and productivity optimization. By identifying the vital few factors that have the most significant impact, one can focus their efforts and resources on what truly matters and maximize efficiency and effectiveness.

3

The Law of Competition

The Law of Competition, often referred to as the principle of competition, is a fundamental concept in economics and business that describes the relationship between firms operating in a market. It is based on the idea that multiple firms competing for the same customers and resources will lead to increased efficiency and improved products or services.

The Law of Competition states that when multiple firms are free to enter a market and compete with each other, they will strive to gain a larger share of the market by offering better products, lower prices, or both. This competition among firms leads to various positive outcomes:

Efficiency: Competition encourages firms to operate more efficiently by reducing costs, improving production techniques, and innovating. Firms are incentivized to find ways to produce goods and services at lower costs to attract customers and increase their market share.

Quality and Innovation: In a competitive market, firms are motivated to improve the quality of their products or services to gain a competitive edge. They invest in research and development, innovation, and technological advancements to differentiate themselves and attract customers.

Consumer Benefits: Competition benefits consumers by offering a wider variety of products, better quality, and lower prices. When firms compete, they are driven to provide more value to consumers to attract and retain them. This leads to increased choices for consumers and often results in lower prices as firms strive to offer the best deals.

Market Regulation: Competition can act as a form of regulation in itself. When firms compete, they need to adhere to market rules and regulations to ensure fair play and avoid unethical or anti-competitive behavior. Competition can prevent monopolistic practices and promote a level playing field.

However, it is important to note that competition also has its challenges and potential negative consequences. Intense competition can lead to market saturation, price wars, and even the exit of less competitive firms. In some cases, competition can be detrimental to smaller businesses that may struggle to compete with larger, more established companies.

To ensure fair competition and protect consumers, governments often enact regulations and antitrust laws to prevent monopolies, collusion, and other anti-competitive practices that can harm market dynamics.

Overall, the Law of Competition serves as a guiding principle in economics, emphasizing the positive effects of competition on efficiency, innovation, quality, and consumer welfare in a market economy.

4

The Law of Innovation

Though,there is no specific "Law of Innovation" that universally defines or governs innovation. However, several principles and concepts are commonly associated with innovation and can be considered guiding principles in the field. Here are a few key ideas that are often discussed in relation to innovation:

Creative Destruction: Coined by economist Joseph Schumpeter, this concept suggests that innovation often involves the creation of new ideas, products, or technologies that render existing ones obsolete. It highlights the disruptive nature of innovation and its potential to reshape industries and economies.

Intellectual Property Laws: Intellectual property (IP) laws, such as patents, copyrights, and trademarks, play a crucial role in fostering innovation. These laws provide legal protection and incentives for creators and inventors, ensuring they can benefit from their innovations and encouraging further innovation.

Moore's Law: Although not specifically focused on innovation, Moore's Law, named after Gordon Moore, co-founder of Intel, states that the number of transistors on a microchip doubles approximately every two years, leading to exponential growth in computing power. This principle has driven rapid technological advancements and innovation in the field of electronics.

Open Innovation: Coined by Henry Chesbrough, open innovation suggests that organizations should actively seek external ideas, expertise, and resources to complement their internal capabilities. It emphasizes collaboration, partnerships, and knowledge-sharing across organizations to accelerate innovation.

Disruptive Innovation: Introduced by Clayton Christensen, the concept of disruptive innovation refers to the development of new products or services that initially serve niche markets or lower-end customers but eventually disrupt established markets or industries. Disruptive innovations often offer new value propositions and fundamentally change the way business is conducted.

It's important to note that while these concepts provide insights into innovation, the nature and laws related to innovation can vary across different countries, industries, and fields of study.

5

The Law of Customer Satisfaction

While there isn't a specific "Law of Customer Satisfaction" that universally governs customer satisfaction, there are several principles and concepts that are commonly associated with it. Customer satisfaction refers to the extent to which customers' expectations and needs are fulfilled by a product, service, or overall experience. Here are some key ideas related to customer satisfaction:

Customer-Centricity: Putting the customer at the center of business decisions and strategies is crucial for achieving customer satisfaction. Understanding customer needs, preferences, and pain points enables organizations to develop products and services that align with their expectations.

Quality and Value: Providing high-quality products or services that deliver value to customers is essential for customer satisfaction. Quality refers to meeting or exceeding customer expectations in terms of performance, reliability, durability, and other relevant factors. Value is the perceived benefits customers receive in relation to the price they pay.

Customer Experience: A positive customer experience is a significant driver of customer satisfaction. It encompasses all interactions and touchpoints a customer has with a brand, including pre-purchase, purchase, and post-purchase stages. Organizations need to focus on delivering seamless, personalized, and delightful experiences throughout the customer journey.

Continuous Improvement: To ensure customer satisfaction, organizations should continuously strive to improve their products, services, and processes. This involves gathering feedback, monitoring customer satisfaction metrics, and implementing changes based on customer insights. A culture of continuous improvement fosters customer loyalty and long-term satisfaction.

Relationship Building: Building strong relationships with customers is crucial for satisfaction and loyalty. This involves proactive communication, providing exceptional customer service, and addressing customer concerns or complaints promptly. Establishing trust and rapport with customers enhances their satisfaction and increases the likelihood of repeat business.

Feedback and Measurement: Regularly seeking customer feedback and measuring satisfaction levels are important for understanding customer perceptions and identifying areas for improvement. Surveys, feedback forms, social listening, and other tools can be utilized to gather insights and track customer satisfaction metrics.

While these principles can contribute to customer satisfaction, it's important to note that customer expectations and satisfaction can vary depending on the industry, product or service, cultural factors, and individual preferences. Organizations need to tailor their approaches to customer satisfaction based on their specific context and customer base.

6

The Law of Leadership
There isn't a specific "Law of Leadership" that universally governs leadership. However, leadership is a complex and multifaceted field with various principles and theories that guide effective leadership practices. Here are some key ideas associated with leadership:

Vision and Direction: Effective leaders provide a clear vision and direction for their teams or organizations. They articulate a compelling future state and inspire others to work towards achieving it. A strong vision helps align and motivate individuals, fostering a sense of purpose and direction.

Influence and Inspiration: Leaders influence others to achieve common goals. They inspire and motivate their team members by setting a positive example, communicating effectively, and encouraging growth and development. Inspirational leadership can create a sense of trust, loyalty, and commitment among followers.

Decision-Making and Problem-Solving: Leaders are responsible for making informed decisions and solving problems. They analyze information, consider alternatives, and make choices that align with organizational goals and values. Effective leaders also involve others in decision-making processes when appropriate, fostering collaboration and ownership.

Communication and Relationship Building: Strong communication skills are vital for effective leadership. Leaders need to convey their expectations, provide feedback, and actively listen to their team members. They also focus on building positive relationships, establishing trust, and fostering a collaborative and inclusive work environment.

Emotional Intelligence: Emotional intelligence refers to the ability to understand and manage emotions, both in oneself and others. Leaders with high emotional intelligence are aware of their own emotions and can empathize with and support the emotions of their team members. This enables them to handle conflicts, build relationships, and inspire others effectively.

Continuous Learning and Development: Leadership is an ongoing journey of learning and growth. Effective leaders actively seek opportunities for self-improvement, acquire new knowledge and skills, and adapt to changing circumstances. They promote a culture of learning and development within their teams and encourage others to enhance their capabilities.

It's important to note that leadership styles and approaches can vary based on the context, organizational culture, and the individuals being led. Different situations may require different leadership styles, such as transformational, democratic, or situational leadership. Successful leaders adapt their approaches based on the needs of their team and the challenges they face.

7

The Law of Cash Flow
The "Law of Cash Flow" is not a specific term or principle commonly used in finance or economics. However, cash flow is a fundamental concept in financial management and refers to the movement of cash into and out of a business or individual's finances over a specific period.

Here are some key principles and concepts related to cash flow management:

Cash Inflows: Cash inflows include revenue from sales, investments, loans, or any other source that brings money into the business or individual's finances. Managing and increasing cash inflows is essential for maintaining liquidity and meeting financial obligations.

Cash Outflows: Cash outflows represent the payments made by a business or individual, including expenses, bills, loan repayments, salaries, and taxes. Managing cash outflows involves controlling expenses, optimizing payment schedules, and prioritizing essential payments.

Cash Flow Statement: A cash flow statement is a financial statement that provides an overview of a business's or individual's cash inflows and outflows during a specific period. It helps assess the liquidity and financial health of the entity and enables effective cash flow management.

Cash Flow Forecasting: Cash flow forecasting involves estimating future cash inflows and outflows to anticipate and plan for potential cash shortages or surpluses. By forecasting cash flow, businesses and individuals can make informed decisions regarding investments, financing, and day-to-day operations.

Working Capital Management: Working capital refers to the funds available to cover day-to-day operations and short-term obligations. Effective working capital management ensures that there is sufficient cash flow to meet operational needs and manage short-term liabilities.

Cash Flow Analysis: Conducting a thorough analysis of cash flow patterns helps identify trends, risks, and opportunities. Analyzing cash flow data can provide insights into the financial performance of a business or individual, highlight areas for improvement, and support strategic decision-making.

Cash Flow Management Strategies: Various strategies can be employed to manage cash flow effectively. These may include maintaining an adequate cash reserve, negotiating favorable payment terms with suppliers, controlling inventory levels, improving collection processes, and considering financing options when necessary.

While there isn't a specific "Law of Cash Flow," managing cash flow is a critical aspect of financial management for both businesses and individuals. Maintaining a healthy cash flow is vital for liquidity, managing financial obligations, and supporting sustainable growth.

8

The Law of Risk and Reward
The "Law of Risk and Reward" is a concept that highlights the relationship between the level of risk undertaken and the potential rewards or returns that can be achieved. It is a fundamental principle in finance and investment. The general idea is that higher levels of risk are typically associated with the potential for higher rewards, while lower levels of risk are associated with lower potential rewards. Here are key points related to the Law of Risk and Reward:

Risk: Risk refers to the uncertainty or probability of experiencing losses or negative outcomes. In the context of investments, it can include market volatility, business performance, economic factors, regulatory changes, and other variables that can affect the value of an investment. Higher-risk investments have a greater chance of loss or negative returns.

Reward: Reward represents the potential gains or positive outcomes that can be achieved from an investment. It can include capital appreciation, income generation, dividends, interest, or other financial benefits. Higher-reward opportunities typically come with a higher level of risk.

Risk-Return Tradeoff: The risk-return tradeoff is the principle that higher potential rewards are generally associated with higher levels of risk. This means that investors or individuals seeking higher returns must be willing to accept a higher degree of risk. Conversely, lower-risk investments tend to offer lower potential returns.

Diversification: Diversification is a risk management strategy that involves spreading investments across different asset classes, industries, or geographic regions. By diversifying, investors aim to reduce the overall risk in their portfolio. Diversification helps balance the potential for higher returns by minimizing the impact of individual investment losses.

Risk Tolerance: Risk tolerance refers to an individual's or entity's willingness and ability to accept and handle risk. It varies depending on factors such as financial goals, time horizon, investment knowledge, and personal preferences. Understanding and evaluating risk tolerance is crucial for making investment decisions that align with one's comfort level.

Risk Management: Risk management involves identifying, assessing, and mitigating risks to minimize potential losses. It includes strategies such as setting appropriate asset allocation, employing risk management tools (e.g., stop-loss orders), conducting thorough research and analysis, and staying informed about market trends and developments.

It's important to note that the relationship between risk and reward is not linear or guaranteed. While higher-risk investments may have the potential for higher rewards, there is also a greater likelihood of incurring losses. It is crucial to carefully evaluate risk-reward profiles, conduct thorough research, and seek professional advice before making investment decisions.

Additionally, individual financial goals, time horizons, and risk tolerance should be considered when determining the appropriate balance between risk and reward. Investment decisions should align with an individual's specific circumstances and preferences.

9

The Law of Marketing

The term "Law of Marketing" does not refer to a specific universally recognized principle or law. However, there are several principles and concepts that guide marketing practices and strategies. These principles help organizations understand and connect with their target audiences, create value, and achieve their marketing objectives. Here are some key ideas related to marketing:

Target Market and Segmentation: Identifying and understanding the target market is essential for effective marketing. Organizations divide their target market into segments based on shared characteristics such as demographics, psychographics, or behaviors. This segmentation allows for targeted marketing efforts tailored to specific customer groups.

Value Creation and Value Proposition: Marketing revolves around creating value for customers. Organizations develop unique value propositions that highlight the benefits and advantages their products or services offer to customers. A strong value proposition differentiates a business from competitors and attracts customers.

Customer Orientation and Relationship Building: Successful marketing is customer-oriented. Organizations focus on building and maintaining positive relationships with customers by understanding their needs, preferences, and feedback. Customer relationship management strategies help foster loyalty, repeat business, and positive word-of-mouth.

Marketing Mix: The marketing mix refers to a set of marketing tactics known as the "4Ps": product, price, place, and promotion. Organizations develop strategies for each element to create a comprehensive marketing plan. This includes decisions about product design, pricing strategies, distribution channels, and promotional activities.

Branding and Positioning: Branding involves creating a unique and recognizable identity for a product, service, or organization. Effective branding establishes an emotional connection with customers and differentiates the offering from competitors. Positioning refers to how an organization positions its product or brand in the minds of consumers, highlighting its unique value and benefits.

Market Research and Analysis: Market research is the process of gathering and analyzing data about customers, competitors, and the overall market environment. It helps organizations understand market trends, customer preferences, and competitive landscapes. Market analysis guides marketing strategies, decision-making, and identifying new opportunities.

Continuous Monitoring and Adaptation: Marketing is an ongoing process that requires continuous monitoring and adaptation. Organizations track marketing metrics, such as sales, customer feedback, and market share, to evaluate the effectiveness of their marketing efforts. They make adjustments and refine their strategies based on market dynamics and customer responses.

It's important to note that the principles and concepts of marketing can vary across industries, contexts, and target markets. Different marketing approaches may be suitable for different products, services, or target audiences. Marketing strategies should be tailored to the specific needs and objectives of the organization and its intended market.

10

The Law of Continuous Learning

The "Law of Continuous Learning" is not a specific term or principle in the traditional sense. However, the concept of continuous learning is widely recognized and embraced across various fields and disciplines. It emphasizes the importance of lifelong learning and the continuous acquisition of knowledge, skills, and personal development. Here are key points related to the idea of continuous learning:

Lifelong Learning: Lifelong learning refers to the belief that learning should continue beyond formal education and throughout one's life. It involves actively seeking new knowledge, skills, and experiences to enhance personal and professional growth.

Adaptation to Change: In today's rapidly changing world, continuous learning is essential for adapting to new technologies, evolving industries, and shifting market dynamics. It enables individuals to stay relevant, agile, and resilient in the face of change.

Professional Development: Continuous learning is crucial for professional development and career advancement. It involves staying updated on industry trends, acquiring new skills and certifications, and expanding one's expertise. This ongoing development enhances job performance and opens up opportunities for growth.

Personal Growth and Well-being: Continuous learning goes beyond professional development. It also encompasses personal growth, self-improvement, and acquiring knowledge in areas of personal interest. Engaging in lifelong learning can enhance one's creativity, critical thinking abilities, and overall well-being.

Information Accessibility: The digital age has made information more accessible than ever before. Online courses, educational platforms, books, podcasts, and other resources provide opportunities for self-directed learning at one's own pace and convenience.

Reflective Practice: Continuous learning involves reflection on past experiences, extracting lessons learned, and applying those insights to future situations. This reflective practice helps individuals refine their skills, identify areas for improvement, and adapt their approaches.

Curiosity and Growth Mindset: Cultivating curiosity and maintaining a growth mindset are key aspects of continuous learning. A growth mindset recognizes that abilities and intelligence can be developed through effort, perseverance, and learning from failures. Embracing curiosity and a growth mindset fosters a lifelong passion for learning.

Learning Communities and Collaboration: Engaging with learning communities, mentorship, and collaborative environments can enhance the learning experience. Interacting with others who share similar interests or expertise provides opportunities for knowledge sharing, feedback, and collective growth.

Continuous learning is a mindset and a commitment to ongoing personal and professional development. It empowers individuals to adapt, innovate, and thrive in a constantly evolving world. By embracing continuous learning, individuals can expand their horizons, unlock new opportunities, and lead fulfilling lives.

11

The Law of Branding
The Law of Branding is a concept that emphasizes the importance of building a strong brand in business. It states that a brand is not simply a logo or a product, but rather the overall perception and reputation that consumers have about a company and its offerings. This perception can be influenced by various factors, including product quality, customer service, advertising, and the company's values and messaging.

The Law of Branding suggests that a well-established and differentiated brand can create a competitive advantage for a company. By effectively communicating its unique value proposition and building strong emotional connections with consumers, a brand can cultivate customer loyalty, increase brand recognition, and command premium pricing.

To comply with the Law of Branding, companies must invest in activities that enhance their brand equity. This involves consistently delivering high-quality products or services, maintaining a positive brand image through marketing and public relations efforts, and ensuring a consistent brand experience across all customer touchpoints.

Building a successful brand requires a deep understanding of the target market, competition analysis, and a strategic approach to brand development and management. Companies need to carefully craft their brand positioning, personality, and messaging to align with the desires and expectations of their target audience.

It's important to note that the Law of Branding applies to both large corporations and small businesses. Regardless of the size of the company, investing in branding can help create a positive perception among consumers and differentiate the business from competitors.

Ultimately, the Law of Branding emphasizes that a brand is an essential asset that can drive long-term business success and create a lasting relationship with customers. By consistently delivering on brand promises and cultivating a strong brand identity, companies can establish a competitive advantage and build customer loyalty in the marketplace.

12

The Law of Differentiation

The Law of Differentiation, also known as the Law of Derivatives, is a fundamental concept in calculus that describes how to find the derivative of a function. The derivative measures the rate at which a quantity is changing with respect to another variable.

In calculus, the derivative of a function $f(x)$ is denoted as $f'(x)$ or dy/dx. It represents the slope of the tangent line to the graph of the function at a specific point. The Law of Differentiation provides a set of rules and formulas to calculate the derivative of various types of functions.

The basic rules of differentiation include:

Power Rule: For a function $f(x) = x^n$, where n is a constant, the derivative is given by $f'(x) = nx^{(n-1)}$. For example, if $f(x) = x^2$, then $f'(x) = 2x$.

Constant Rule: The derivative of a constant C is always zero. If $f(x) = C$, then $f'(x) = 0$.

Sum/Difference Rule: For two functions $f(x)$ and $g(x)$, the derivative of their sum or difference is equal to the sum or difference of their derivatives. If $f(x)$ and $g(x)$ are differentiable functions, then $(f(x) \pm g(x))' = f'(x) \pm g'(x)$.

Product Rule: For two functions $f(x)$ and $g(x)$, the derivative of their product is given by $(f(x)g(x))' = f'(x)g(x) + f(x)g'(x)$.

Quotient Rule: For two functions $f(x)$ and $g(x)$, where $g(x) \neq 0$, the derivative of their quotient is given by $(f(x)/g(x))' = (f'(x)g(x) - f(x)g'(x))/[g(x)]^2$.

Chain Rule: The chain rule is used to find the derivative of composite functions. If $y = f(g(x))$, then $dy/dx = f'(g(x)) * g'(x)$.

These are some of the fundamental rules of differentiation that are used to calculate derivatives in calculus. The Law of Differentiation plays a crucial role in various areas of mathematics, physics, engineering, and other fields where rates of change and slopes are important.

13

The Law of Cost-Benefit Analysis
Cost-benefit analysis (CBA) is a systematic process used to evaluate the pros and cons of a decision or project by comparing its costs and benefits. It is a fundamental principle in economics and decision-making that helps individuals, businesses, and governments assess the potential outcomes and make informed choices.

The law of cost-benefit analysis is not a formal term or principle but rather a general concept that underlies the practice of CBA. It can be understood as follows:

Every decision or action involves costs and benefits: The law of cost-benefit analysis recognizes that every choice we make, whether personal or societal, has associated costs and benefits. Costs refer to the resources, such as money, time, and effort, required to implement a decision, while benefits represent the positive outcomes or gains resulting from that decision.

Costs and benefits are subjective: The perception of costs and benefits can vary among individuals or groups. What may be considered a cost to one person may be a benefit to another. For example, the cost of purchasing a car may be a burden to someone on a tight budget, while it can be viewed as a benefit to someone who needs reliable transportation.

Costs and benefits are not always monetary: While financial considerations are often a significant aspect of cost-benefit analysis, costs and benefits can extend beyond monetary terms. They can include social, environmental, and intangible factors that are challenging to quantify but still play a role in decision-making. For instance, the impact of a new infrastructure project on the environment or the quality of life in a community.

Comparative analysis is essential: The law of cost-benefit analysis emphasizes the importance of comparing costs and benefits. It involves evaluating the costs and benefits of different options or scenarios and determining which one provides the greatest overall benefit, given the associated costs. This comparative analysis enables decision-makers to prioritize options and allocate resources efficiently.

Rational decision-making is based on net benefits: The goal of cost-benefit analysis is to identify the option or project that maximizes net benefits. Net benefits are calculated by subtracting the total costs from the total benefits. Rational decision-making suggests that individuals or organizations should choose the option with the highest net benefits, as it indicates the most favorable outcome.

It is important to note that the law of cost-benefit analysis does not prescribe a specific approach or formula for conducting the analysis. Various methodologies and techniques can be employed depending on the context and nature of the decision. Nevertheless, the overarching principle remains the same: weighing the costs against the benefits to make informed choices that optimize outcomes.

14

The Law of Scalability

In the context of business, the term "Law of Scalability" is not a widely recognized or established principle like some other well-known business laws (e.g., Moore's Law in technology). However, the concept of scalability is highly relevant and crucial for businesses to thrive and grow.

In business, scalability refers to the ability of a company or organization to handle increased demands, growth, or expansion without compromising efficiency or quality. It involves designing business models, processes, and systems that can adapt and accommodate larger volumes of customers, transactions, or operations.

Here are some key considerations related to scalability in business:

Infrastructure: A scalable business needs to have the necessary infrastructure in place to handle growth. This includes physical resources like manufacturing facilities or data centers, as well as technology infrastructure such as servers, networks, and software systems.

Processes: Scalable businesses have well-defined and streamlined processes that can be replicated and scaled up as needed. This involves developing efficient workflows, standardized procedures, and automated systems to handle increased volumes efficiently.

Flexibility: Scalable businesses are adaptable and can respond to changing market conditions, customer needs, or industry trends. This may involve diversifying product or service offerings, entering new markets, or adjusting strategies based on emerging opportunities or challenges.

Scalable Business Models: Some business models inherently lend themselves to scalability. For example, subscription-based models, software-as-a-service (SaaS), or online marketplaces can be designed to handle a growing user base or transaction volume without significant increases in resources or costs.

Talent and Skills: As a business scales, having the right talent and skills becomes crucial. Hiring and developing a capable workforce, empowering employees to take on new responsibilities, and fostering a culture of innovation and continuous improvement are essential for scalability.

Customer Focus: Scalable businesses prioritize customer satisfaction and focus on building strong customer relationships. This includes delivering high-quality products or services, providing excellent customer support, and actively seeking feedback to drive continuous improvement.

While there may not be a specific "Law of Scalability" in business, the concept is fundamental for companies aiming to achieve sustainable growth and success. By strategically planning for scalability, businesses can position themselves to handle increasing demands, seize opportunities, and stay competitive in their respective markets.

15

The Law of Adaptability

The concept of adaptability is indeed crucial in the business world. It refers to a company's ability to respond and adjust to changes in its internal and external environment. Here are a few key points related to adaptability in the context of business:

Flexibility: Businesses need to be flexible and open to change. This involves being willing to modify strategies, processes, products, and services in response to evolving market conditions, customer preferences, technological advancements, and competitive pressures.

Innovation: Adaptability often goes hand in hand with innovation. Businesses that embrace innovation continually seek new ways to improve their operations, develop new products or services, and explore untapped markets. They proactively adapt to market trends and anticipate future needs.

Agility: An agile business is capable of quickly and efficiently adapting to changes. This includes being able to make decisions promptly, allocate resources effectively, and adjust operations or strategies as required. Agile businesses are often more responsive to customer demands and better positioned to seize new opportunities.

Learning Orientation: Adaptability in business involves fostering a learning culture within the organization. This means encouraging employees to acquire new skills, promoting knowledge sharing, and embracing a mindset of continuous improvement. Businesses that prioritize learning can adapt more effectively to changes and stay ahead in a rapidly evolving marketplace.

Resilience: Adaptability is closely linked to resilience. Resilient businesses have the capacity to bounce back from setbacks, navigate challenges, and recover from disruptions. They anticipate potential risks, have contingency plans in place, and can adapt swiftly when unexpected circumstances arise.

While the term "Law of Adaptability" may not be a widely recognized term in business literature, the concept itself is highly relevant and acknowledged as a vital factor for success in the ever-changing business landscape.

16

The Law of Decision Making
The term "Law of Decision Making" is not a specific or widely recognized legal principle or concept. However, there are various legal frameworks, principles, and theories that relate to decision making in different contexts. Here are a few general principles and theories that can guide decision making within the legal system:

Legal Principles: Legal systems typically adhere to fundamental principles such as fairness, justice, equality, and the rule of law. These principles are intended to guide decision making by ensuring that decisions are made in a just and impartial manner.

Due Process: The concept of due process requires that individuals be given fair and reasonable procedures before any significant decisions are made that may affect their rights, liberties, or interests. This principle aims to ensure that decision making is transparent, unbiased, and based on reliable evidence.

Precedent: Many legal systems follow the principle of stare decisis, which means that decisions made in earlier cases should be followed as precedents in similar subsequent cases. This principle helps provide consistency and predictability in decision making by relying on established legal principles and interpretations.

Balancing Tests: In some areas of law, decision making involves weighing competing interests or rights. Courts may employ balancing tests to assess and compare the various factors at play and make a determination that strikes a fair balance between conflicting considerations.

Rational Decision Making: Decision making in the legal context often relies on rational analysis and reasoning. Judges, juries, and legal professionals are expected to consider relevant facts, evidence, legal principles, and arguments before arriving at a decision. Rational decision making aims to ensure that decisions are logical, coherent, and based on a sound understanding of the law.

It is important to note that decision making within the legal system can vary depending on the jurisdiction, specific area of law, and the nature of the decision being made. Legal systems may have their own specific rules, procedures, and doctrines that govern decision making within their respective contexts.

17

The Law of Teamwork

In a business context, "The Law of Teamwork" typically refers to the idea that effective teamwork is essential for achieving success and maximizing performance within an organization. It emphasizes the importance of collaboration, coordination, and synergy among team members. While it is not a legally binding principle, it highlights the critical role that teamwork plays in driving business outcomes. Here are some key aspects of "The Law of Teamwork" in the business world:

Common goals: A strong team in a business setting works towards a shared vision and common goals. This shared purpose provides a sense of direction and alignment, ensuring that everyone is working together towards a unified objective.

Clear communication: Effective communication is crucial for successful teamwork. Team members should be able to express their ideas, concerns, and expectations openly and honestly. Clear and transparent communication helps in avoiding misunderstandings, resolving conflicts, and ensuring that everyone is on the same page.

Role clarity: Each team member should have a clear understanding of their roles and responsibilities within the team. Defining roles helps in maximizing efficiency, avoiding duplication of efforts, and ensuring that tasks are assigned to the most suitable individuals based on their skills and expertise.

Trust and collaboration: Trust is the foundation of effective teamwork. Team members need to trust and rely on each other's abilities, judgment, and commitment. Collaboration involves actively working together, leveraging each other's strengths, and pooling resources to achieve the desired outcomes.

Diversity and inclusion: Embracing diversity in a team can lead to better problem-solving and decision-making. Teams that incorporate individuals with different backgrounds, experiences, and perspectives can bring fresh ideas, innovative solutions, and a broader range of insights to the table.

Support and accountability: Team members should support and help one another to foster a positive and productive work environment. At the same time, there should be a sense of individual and collective accountability for meeting deadlines, delivering quality work, and achieving team goals.

Continuous improvement: Teams should encourage a culture of learning and continuous improvement. This involves reflecting on past experiences, analyzing successes and failures, and implementing lessons learned to enhance performance and drive innovation.

By adhering to "The Law of Teamwork" in business, organizations can harness the collective potential of their employees, enhance productivity, and foster a positive work culture. Effective teamwork can lead to increased efficiency, improved decision-making, higher employee satisfaction, and ultimately contribute to the success and growth of the business.

18

The Law of Delegation

The Law of Delegation is a principle that emphasizes the importance of effectively assigning tasks and responsibilities to others within an organization or group. It is based on the notion that leaders and managers should not try to do everything themselves but instead distribute tasks among their subordinates to achieve greater efficiency and productivity.

The concept of delegation is rooted in the understanding that leaders have a finite amount of time and resources, and by delegating tasks, they can focus on higher-level responsibilities and strategic decision-making. Delegation not only empowers subordinates but also enables them to develop new skills and gain valuable experience.

The Law of Delegation involves several key principles:

Authority: When delegating tasks, leaders must delegate the necessary authority to complete those tasks. This includes granting decision-making power and providing the required resources and support.

Responsibility: While leaders delegate tasks, they cannot delegate ultimate responsibility. The person to whom a task is delegated becomes responsible for its completion, but the leader remains accountable for the outcome.

Clear Communication: Delegation requires clear and effective communication. The leader should clearly explain the task, its objectives, deadlines, and any specific guidelines or expectations.

Competence and Development: Delegation should be based on the competence and skills of individuals. Leaders must assess the abilities of their subordinates and delegate tasks accordingly. Additionally, delegation can be an opportunity for skill development and growth, allowing subordinates to take on new challenges and expand their capabilities.

Monitoring and Feedback: Leaders should establish mechanisms for monitoring progress and providing feedback to the individuals to whom tasks are delegated. This helps ensure that tasks are on track, provides opportunities for clarification or guidance, and enables continuous improvement.

By following the Law of Delegation, leaders can foster a more efficient and productive work environment, empower their team members, and focus on strategic initiatives that drive organizational success.

19

The Law of Time Management
The term law of time management is commonly used to refer to the principles and practices that help individuals effectively manage their time and achieve their goals. Time management is crucial for personal productivity, reducing stress, and maximizing efficiency. Here are some key principles often associated with effective time management:

Setting Priorities: Determine what tasks and activities are most important and align them with your goals and values. Prioritizing helps you focus your time and energy on what truly matters.

Goal Setting: Clearly define your short-term and long-term goals. This provides a roadmap for your activities and allows you to allocate your time accordingly.

Planning and Scheduling: Create a plan or schedule that outlines your tasks, deadlines, and appointments. Utilize tools such as calendars, to-do lists, or digital productivity apps to help organize and allocate your time effectively.

Time Allocation: Allocate your time based on the importance and urgency of tasks. Differentiate between essential, non-essential, and time-wasting activities. Consider the 80/20 rule (Pareto Principle), which suggests that 80% of your results come from 20% of your efforts. Focus on high-impact tasks that yield significant results.

Time Blocking: Group similar tasks or activities together and allocate specific time blocks for them. This reduces distractions and allows for dedicated focus on specific types of work.

Eliminating Time Wasters: Identify and minimize or eliminate activities that consume excessive time without adding significant value. Examples include excessive social media use, unnecessary meetings, or procrastination.

Delegation and Outsourcing: Delegate tasks that can be handled by others, freeing up your time for more important responsibilities. Outsourcing certain activities or using automation tools can also save time.

Effective Communication: Clear and concise communication helps avoid misunderstandings, prevents unnecessary back-and-forth, and saves time in both personal and professional interactions.

Avoiding Multitasking: While multitasking may seem efficient, it can often lead to decreased productivity and quality of work. Focus on one task at a time to maximize concentration and effectiveness.

Time for Self-Care: Make time for relaxation, breaks, and self-care activities. Taking care of your physical and mental well-being helps maintain productivity and prevents burnout.

Remember, time management is a personal skill that requires experimentation and adaptation to find what works best for you. Different strategies and techniques may be more effective in different situations, so it's important to continuously assess and adjust your approach to time management.

20

The Law of Integrity
The Law of Integrity is a principle that emphasizes the importance of acting in accordance with strong moral and ethical principles. It revolves around the idea of being honest, trustworthy, and consistent in one's actions and behavior. Integrity is a fundamental aspect of personal and professional conduct, and it forms the foundation of trust and credibility in relationships.

Here are some key aspects of the Law of Integrity:

Honesty: Acting with integrity involves being truthful and sincere in all interactions. It means being honest with oneself and with others, even when faced with difficult or uncomfortable situations.

Consistency: Demonstrating consistency in behavior and actions is essential for integrity. It means aligning one's words and actions, and following through on commitments and promises.

Accountability: Taking responsibility for one's actions and their consequences is a crucial aspect of integrity. It involves owning up to mistakes, admitting when wrong, and making amends or taking appropriate corrective actions.

Trustworthiness: Being trustworthy is central to integrity. It means being reliable, dependable, and maintaining confidentiality when required. Trust is built over time through consistent and honorable conduct.

Ethical Behavior: Upholding ethical standards and principles is integral to acting with integrity. It involves making decisions and taking actions that are fair, just, and respectful of others. Ethical behavior takes into account the rights, welfare, and well-being of individuals and the broader community.

Authenticity: Being authentic and true to oneself is a key aspect of integrity. It means living in alignment with one's values and beliefs, even when facing challenges or pressures to compromise them.

Transparency: Acting with transparency involves being open and honest in communication and decision-making processes. It means providing information, sharing intentions, and seeking input from others when appropriate.

Professionalism: Demonstrating professionalism in all endeavors is an essential part of integrity. It involves maintaining high standards of conduct, respecting others, and adhering to professional codes of ethics.

Leading by Example: Individuals who embody integrity serve as role models for others. They inspire trust and encourage others to act with integrity through their own consistent and ethical behavior.

Self-Reflection and Growth: Practicing integrity requires ongoing self-reflection and a commitment to personal growth. It involves examining one's beliefs, values, and actions, and striving to improve and align them with the principles of integrity.

By embracing the Law of Integrity, individuals can build strong relationships, foster trust, and maintain a solid reputation. Acting with integrity is not always easy, but it is a fundamental aspect of personal and professional success and contributes to a positive and ethical society.

21

The Law of Ethical Conduct
In the context of business, the "Law of Ethical Conduct" typically refers to a set of principles, guidelines, and legal frameworks that govern ethical behavior in the business environment. While there isn't a singular law by that name, there are various laws, regulations, and ethical principles that businesses are expected to adhere to. Here are some key aspects related to the law of ethical conduct in business:

Legal Compliance: Businesses are required to comply with a range of laws and regulations that govern their operations. This includes areas such as labor laws, environmental regulations, consumer protection laws, intellectual property rights, and more. Adhering to these laws is a fundamental aspect of ethical conduct in business.

Fair Competition: Ethical business conduct promotes fair competition and prohibits anti-competitive practices such as price-fixing, collusion, market manipulation, or unfair trade practices. Laws and regulations related to competition, such as antitrust laws, aim to ensure a level playing field and prevent the abuse of market power.

Transparency and Accountability: Ethical businesses strive for transparency in their operations, financial reporting, and communication with stakeholders. This includes providing accurate and timely information, avoiding conflicts of interest, and maintaining proper accounting practices. Various laws, such as securities regulations and corporate governance requirements, promote transparency and accountability in business.

Ethical Marketing and Advertising: Businesses are expected to engage in truthful and responsible marketing and advertising practices. This involves avoiding false or misleading claims, respecting consumer privacy, and adhering to advertising standards set by regulatory bodies. Laws and regulations related to advertising and consumer protection govern these practices.

Employee Rights and Welfare: Ethical conduct in business involves respecting and safeguarding the rights and welfare of employees. This includes fair treatment, non-discrimination, providing a safe and healthy work environment, paying fair wages, and ensuring reasonable working hours. Labor laws and regulations address many of these aspects.

Social and Environmental Responsibility: Ethical businesses consider their impact on society and the environment. They strive to minimize negative effects and may actively engage in corporate social responsibility initiatives, sustainable practices, and philanthropy. While not legally mandated in all jurisdictions, many companies voluntarily adopt socially and environmentally responsible practices.

It's important to note that the specific laws and regulations governing ethical conduct in business can vary across countries and jurisdictions. Businesses should familiarize themselves with the legal frameworks applicable to their industry and location, and consult legal professionals or experts for advice on compliance. Additionally, industry-specific codes of conduct and ethical guidelines may exist to further promote responsible business practices.

22

The Law of Transparency

The term "Law of Transparency" is not a universally recognized or established legal principle. However, it can be used to refer to the concept of transparency in governance, law, or business practices. Transparency generally refers to the openness, clarity, and accessibility of information, processes, and decision-making.

In the context of governance, the principle of transparency emphasizes the need for government institutions and officials to operate in a manner that allows public scrutiny and accountability. It involves making information about government policies, actions, and expenditures readily available to the public. Transparency in governance helps to foster trust, prevent corruption, and ensure that decisions are made in the best interest of the public.

In the legal context, transparency can refer to the accessibility and comprehensibility of laws and legal processes. It involves ensuring that laws are written in a clear and understandable manner, and that legal proceedings are conducted in an open and impartial manner. Transparent legal systems are essential for upholding the rule of law, ensuring equal access to justice, and promoting public confidence in the legal system.

In business practices, transparency is often associated with the disclosure of information about a company's operations, finances, and ethical practices. Transparent business practices involve providing accurate and complete information to stakeholders, including shareholders, employees, customers, and the public. Transparency in business is crucial for building trust, attracting investment, and maintaining a positive reputation.

While the Law of Transparency may not be a specific legal principle, the concept of transparency is recognized as an important value in many legal systems and governance frameworks. It promotes accountability, integrity, and trust in various spheres of society, and it is often supported by laws and regulations that require the disclosure of information and the protection of whistleblowers.

23

The Law of Trust

The law of trust in business refers to the legal framework that governs the establishment and operation of trust relationships within a business context. A trust is a legal arrangement in which one party (the trustor or settlor) transfers ownership or control of certain assets to another party (the trustee) for the benefit of a third party (the beneficiary). Trusts are commonly used in business for various purposes, including asset protection, estate planning, and investment management.

The law of trust in business encompasses several key principles and concepts:

Trust Formation: To create a trust, the trustor must express an intention to create a trust, identify the assets to be transferred into the trust, name the trustee, and designate the beneficiaries. This is typically done through a written trust agreement or declaration.

Fiduciary Duty: The trustee has a fiduciary duty to act in the best interests of the beneficiaries. This duty requires the trustee to manage the trust assets prudently, avoid conflicts of interest, and act in good faith.

Trust Administration: The trustee is responsible for administering the trust in accordance with the terms set forth in the trust agreement. This includes managing the trust assets, distributing income or principal to the beneficiaries as specified, and maintaining accurate records.

Duty of Loyalty: The trustee must act loyally and solely in the interests of the beneficiaries. This means avoiding self-dealing, conflicts of interest, and any actions that could compromise the beneficiaries' interests.

Duty of Care: The trustee is obligated to exercise reasonable care and skill in managing the trust assets. This involves prudently investing and managing the assets, staying informed about market conditions, and making informed decisions.

Trustee Liability: Trustees can be held personally liable for breaching their fiduciary duties. Beneficiaries or other interested parties can take legal action to seek damages or removal of the trustee if they believe the trustee has acted improperly or negligently.

Trustee Succession: Trust agreements may specify provisions for trustee succession, such as appointing successor trustees in case the original trustee becomes incapacitated or unable to fulfill their duties.

Trust Termination: Trusts may have a specific termination date or be designed to continue for an indefinite period. Upon termination, the trust assets are distributed to the beneficiaries as outlined in the trust agreement.

It's important to note that the specific laws governing trusts can vary between jurisdictions. Different countries may have different trust laws, so it is crucial to consult with legal professionals familiar with the relevant jurisdiction's laws when establishing or managing a trust in a business context.

24

The Law of Collaboration
There are several laws, principles, and frameworks related to collaboration and teamwork in business, but they are typically referred to by different names.

However, in a broader sense, collaboration in business is guided by certain principles and best practices that can be considered as "laws" of collaboration. These principles include:

Shared Vision and Goals: Successful collaboration requires a shared vision and common goals among all parties involved. This helps align efforts and ensures everyone is working towards the same objectives.

Clear Communication: Effective communication is crucial for collaboration. Clear and open communication fosters understanding, reduces misunderstandings, and enables effective coordination and cooperation.

Trust and Mutual Respect: Collaboration thrives in an environment of trust and mutual respect. Building trust among collaborators is essential for open dialogue, idea sharing, and effective decision-making.

Defined Roles and Responsibilities: Clearly defining roles and responsibilities within a collaborative effort helps avoid confusion, duplication of efforts, and ensures accountability.

Flexibility and Adaptability: Collaboration often requires flexibility and adaptability to accommodate different perspectives, changing circumstances, and evolving needs. Being open to new ideas and approaches is essential for successful collaboration.

Conflict Resolution: Collaboration can sometimes lead to conflicts or disagreements. Establishing processes and strategies for resolving conflicts in a constructive manner is important to maintain healthy working relationships.

Celebrate Diversity: Collaboration benefits from diverse perspectives, skills, and experiences. Embracing diversity and inclusivity allows for innovative thinking and more robust problem-solving.

While these principles are not specific laws in the legal sense, they are widely recognized as key factors for successful collaboration in business. By following these principles, organizations can enhance their collaborative efforts and achieve better results.

25

The Law of Partnerships
The Law of Partnerships refers to the legal framework that governs the formation, operation, and dissolution of partnerships. A partnership is a business structure where two or more individuals or entities come together to carry on a business for profit. The laws surrounding partnerships vary by jurisdiction, but there are general principles and legal provisions that apply to partnerships in many countries. Here are some key aspects of partnership law:

Formation: Partnerships are typically formed through an agreement between the partners, either through an oral or written partnership agreement. The agreement outlines the rights, obligations, and responsibilities of each partner, including profit-sharing, decision-making authority, and contributions to the partnership.

Joint and Several Liability: One significant characteristic of partnerships is that partners have joint and several liability. This means that each partner is individually liable for the partnership's debts and obligations. In other words, partners can be held personally responsible for the partnership's debts, even if they were not directly involved in incurring those debts.

Shared Profits and Losses: Partnerships distribute profits and losses among the partners according to the agreed-upon terms in the partnership agreement. The partnership agreement typically outlines the profit-sharing ratio, which determines how the profits will be divided among the partners.

Fiduciary Duties: Partners owe fiduciary duties to one another and to the partnership itself. Fiduciary duties include obligations of loyalty, good faith, and acting in the best interest of the partnership. Partners must avoid conflicts of interest and act in a manner that promotes the success of the partnership.

Partnership Property: Partnerships can own property, enter into contracts, and conduct business activities in their own name. However, partnership property is considered separate from the individual assets of the partners.

Dissolution: Partnerships can be dissolved through various means, such as expiration of a fixed term, agreement of the partners, or by court order. Upon dissolution, the partnership's assets are typically liquidated, and the debts and obligations are settled before distributing any remaining assets among the partners.

It's important to note that partnership laws may differ in various jurisdictions, and it's advisable to consult with legal professionals who specialize in partnership law in your specific jurisdiction to understand the precise legal requirements and implications of forming and operating a partnership.

26

The Law of Networking
The term "Law of Networking" is not a specific legal term or principle. However, networking is a common practice in the business world that refers to building relationships, making connections, and fostering professional contacts. While there might not be a legal framework specifically designated as the "Law of Networking," there are general principles and best practices that can guide effective networking. Here are some key considerations:

Building Relationships: Networking is about establishing and nurturing relationships with others. It's essential to approach networking with a genuine interest in others and a willingness to help and support them.

Reciprocity: Networking is a two-way street. It involves giving and receiving support, advice, and opportunities. By offering assistance and value to others, you build goodwill and create a foundation for mutually beneficial relationships.

Authenticity and Trust: Be authentic in your interactions and strive to build trust with others. Trust is a vital element in successful networking, as it facilitates open communication, collaboration, and opportunities for collaboration.

Effective Communication: Communication skills play a crucial role in networking. Be an active listener, ask meaningful questions, and convey your ideas and expertise clearly and concisely. Effective communication helps establish rapport and understanding with others.

Building a Diverse Network: Aim to connect with individuals from diverse backgrounds, industries, and areas of expertise. A diverse network provides access to different perspectives, knowledge, and opportunities.

Leveraging Technology: In today's digital age, networking extends beyond in-person interactions. Utilize online platforms, such as professional networking sites and social media, to expand your network and maintain connections.

Follow-Up and Follow-Through: After networking events or meetings, follow up with the individuals you've connected with. Send a personalized message, express gratitude, and find ways to continue the conversation or provide support. Consistently follow through on any commitments or promises you make during networking interactions.

While not legally binding, these principles can contribute to building meaningful professional relationships and expanding your network. Networking is a dynamic and ongoing process, so it's important to invest time and effort into maintaining and nurturing your connections over time.

27

The Law of Negotiation

The "Law of Negotiation" is not a specific legal term or principle. However, negotiation is a fundamental aspect of business and everyday life. It involves a process of discussion and compromise aimed at reaching mutually acceptable agreements between two or more parties. While negotiation does not have strict legal rules, there are general principles and strategies that can guide effective negotiation. Here are some key considerations:

Preparation: Adequate preparation is crucial for successful negotiation. Understand your objectives, gather relevant information, identify your strengths and weaknesses, and anticipate potential outcomes and alternatives.

Clear Communication: Effective communication is essential in negotiation. Clearly express your position, listen actively to the other party's perspective, ask clarifying questions, and strive for mutual understanding.

Win-Win Approach: Aim for a win-win outcome, where both parties feel they have achieved their objectives and gained value from the negotiation. Look for creative solutions that address the interests of all parties involved.

Flexibility and Compromise: Negotiation often requires flexibility and willingness to compromise. Be open to alternative proposals and explore options that can satisfy the needs and priorities of both sides.

Focus on Interests, Not Positions: Instead of solely focusing on fixed positions, try to understand the underlying interests and motivations of all parties. By identifying common interests, it becomes easier to find mutually beneficial solutions.

Problem-Solving Orientation: Approach negotiation as a problem-solving exercise rather than a confrontational battle. Collaborate with the other party to identify shared goals and brainstorm potential solutions.

Patience and Persistence: Negotiation can be a complex process that requires patience and persistence. Be prepared for setbacks, be willing to explore different options, and maintain a positive attitude throughout the process.

Documentation: Once an agreement is reached, it is advisable to document the terms in writing. This helps ensure clarity and prevents misunderstandings or disputes later on.

While negotiation principles are not legally binding, they can guide individuals in achieving positive outcomes and reaching agreements. It's important to note that legal regulations and contractual obligations may apply to specific negotiations, and consulting legal professionals or experts in the relevant field can provide guidance on legal requirements and implications in specific situations.

The "Law of Negotiation in Business" is not a specific legal term or principle. However, negotiation is a critical skill and process in business transactions, partnerships, contracts, and various other aspects of the business world. While negotiation does not have strict legal rules, there are general principles and strategies that can guide effective negotiation in a business context. Here are some key considerations:

Preparation: Adequate preparation is crucial for successful business negotiation. Understand your goals and objectives, research the other party's position and interests, gather relevant information, and develop a clear negotiation strategy.

Know Your Value: Understand the value of what you are offering or seeking in the negotiation. Determine your leverage points and be prepared to articulate and defend your value proposition.

Establish Clear Objectives: Define your desired outcomes and objectives for the negotiation. Be specific about what you want to achieve and prioritize your goals.

Understand the Other Party: Gain insights into the interests, needs, and motivations of the other party. Understand their perspective, constraints, and potential areas of flexibility.

Build Rapport and Trust: Building rapport and trust with the other party can foster a positive negotiation environment. Effective communication, active listening, and finding common ground can help establish trust and improve the chances of reaching mutually beneficial agreements.

Seek Win-Win Solutions: Aim for outcomes that are beneficial to both parties involved. Look for creative solutions that address the interests and concerns of both sides.

Effective Communication: Communication plays a crucial role in business negotiation. Clearly articulate your position, actively listen to the other party, ask clarifying questions, and strive for mutual understanding.

Flexibility and Compromise: Business negotiation often requires flexibility and the willingness to make compromises. Be open to alternative proposals and explore options that can satisfy the needs and priorities of both parties.

Document Agreements: Once an agreement is reached, it is essential to document the terms in writing. This helps ensure clarity and serves as a reference point for both parties in the future.

Professionalism and Ethical Conduct: Maintain professionalism and adhere to ethical standards throughout the negotiation process. Conduct negotiations in good faith, avoid deceptive practices, and honor commitments made during the negotiation.

While negotiation principles are not legally binding, they can significantly impact the outcomes and success of business negotiations. It's important to note that specific legal requirements, contractual obligations, and regulations may apply in certain business negotiations, and consulting legal professionals or experts in the relevant field is advisable to ensure compliance and protect your interests.

28

The Law of Sales

In a business context, "The Law of Sales" generally refers to the legal principles and regulations that govern commercial sales transactions. These laws ensure that business sales are conducted fairly, protect the rights of both buyers and sellers, and provide remedies in case of disputes or breaches of contract. Here are some key aspects of the law of sales in business:

Contract Formation: Businesses enter into sales contracts through a process of offer, acceptance, and consideration. The terms of the contract, including the quantity, price, delivery terms, and payment terms, should be clearly agreed upon by both parties.

Uniform Commercial Code (UCC): The UCC, which has been adopted in whole or in part by all U.S. states, provides a standardized set of rules for sales transactions involving goods. It addresses matters such as contract formation, warranties, risk of loss, and remedies for breach of contract.

Terms and Conditions: Businesses often include terms and conditions in their sales contracts or on their invoices. These terms can cover matters such as payment terms, delivery terms, limitations of liability, and dispute resolution mechanisms. It is important for businesses to ensure that their terms and conditions are properly communicated to the other party and agreed upon.

Warranties: Businesses may provide warranties or guarantees regarding the quality, performance, or fitness for a particular purpose of the goods being sold. These warranties can be express (explicitly stated) or implied (imposed by law). The law provides remedies for breaches of warranties, including potential liability for damages.

Title and Risk of Loss: The law determines when ownership and the risk of loss transfer from the seller to the buyer. It is essential for businesses to clearly establish when the responsibility for the goods passes to the buyer, as this affects issues such as delivery, insurance, and liability.

Product Liability: Businesses selling products have a legal obligation to ensure that their products are safe for consumers. Product liability laws hold businesses accountable for injuries or damages caused by defective or unsafe products. These laws vary between jurisdictions but often impose strict liability or require proof of negligence.

Consumer Protection Laws: Businesses engaged in sales to consumers are subject to specific consumer protection laws. These laws prohibit deceptive practices, unfair trade practices, false advertising, and other forms of consumer exploitation. They often provide consumers with additional rights and remedies in sales transactions.

Remedies for Breach of Contract: If either party fails to fulfill its obligations under a sales contract, the law provides remedies for the aggrieved party. These remedies may include monetary damages, specific performance, termination of the contract, or other forms of relief.

It's important for businesses to have a solid understanding of the relevant laws and regulations governing sales transactions in their jurisdiction. Consulting with legal professionals specializing in business and commercial law is advisable to ensure compliance and protect the rights and interests of the business in sales transactions.

29

The Law of Pricing
The term "The Law of Pricing" does not refer to a specific legal principle or regulation. However, pricing in business is influenced by

various legal, economic, and market factors. Let's explore some key considerations related to pricing in a business context:

Competition Law: Pricing practices may be subject to competition laws, which aim to prevent anti-competitive behavior and maintain fair competition in the marketplace. Laws against price fixing, collusion, predatory pricing, and abuse of dominant market position can impact pricing strategies.

Price Discrimination: Price discrimination refers to the practice of charging different prices to different customers for the same product or service. Some jurisdictions have laws or regulations that restrict or prohibit unfair or discriminatory pricing practices.

Price Advertising: Laws and regulations govern how prices are advertised to consumers. These rules may require clear and accurate pricing information, disclosure of additional fees or charges, and restrictions on misleading or deceptive pricing practices.

Minimum Pricing Laws: In certain industries or for specific products, governments may establish minimum pricing laws to protect businesses from unfair competition or to address public health concerns. These laws set a minimum price floor that businesses must adhere to.

Contractual Agreements: Businesses may negotiate and enter into contractual agreements with customers, suppliers, or distributors that include pricing terms. These agreements define the pricing structure, payment terms, and any discounts or incentives.

Cost Considerations: Pricing decisions are often influenced by various cost factors, such as production costs, raw material costs, labor costs, overhead expenses, and desired profit margins. It is important to ensure that pricing is set at a level that covers costs and allows for a reasonable profit.

Market Factors: Pricing strategies also need to consider market dynamics, such as supply and demand, competitive landscape, customer preferences, and pricing elasticity. Market research and analysis can help inform pricing decisions to maximize sales and profitability.

Price Changes and Flexibility: Businesses may need to adjust prices over time due to changing market conditions, cost fluctuations, or other factors. However, it's important to comply with any contractual obligations and legal requirements when implementing price changes.

It is crucial for businesses to be aware of the legal and regulatory frameworks that may impact pricing decisions in their specific industry and jurisdiction. Consulting with legal professionals or industry experts can provide guidance on pricing practices and help ensure compliance with applicable laws and regulations.

30

The Law of Revenue Generation

The term "Law of Revenue Generation" is not a widely recognized or established concept in the field of business or economics. However, revenue generation refers to the process of generating income or sales for a business or organization. While there are no specific laws governing revenue generation, there are various principles and strategies that businesses follow to generate revenue effectively. Here are some key factors that contribute to revenue generation:

Product or Service Quality: Providing high-quality products or services that meet customer needs and expectations is essential for revenue generation. When customers are satisfied with their purchases, they are more likely to become repeat customers and recommend the business to others.

Market Demand: Understanding market demand is crucial for revenue generation. Businesses need to identify target markets, analyze consumer preferences, and develop products or services that align with market needs. By offering something that customers want, businesses can attract more buyers and generate revenue.

Pricing Strategy: Setting the right prices for products or services is vital for revenue generation. Businesses need to consider factors such as production costs, competition, and customer value perception. Pricing too high may deter customers, while pricing too low may result in lower profit margins. Finding the optimal balance is crucial.

Marketing and Promotion: Effective marketing and promotion strategies are essential for revenue generation. Businesses need to create awareness about their products or services and convince potential customers to make a purchase. This can be done through various channels, such as advertising, social media, public relations, and targeted marketing campaigns.

Customer Relationship Management: Building strong relationships with customers can lead to increased revenue. By providing excellent customer service, addressing concerns, and maintaining regular communication, businesses can enhance customer satisfaction and loyalty. Loyal customers are more likely to continue buying from the business and may even become brand advocates.

Innovation and Adaptation: In today's rapidly changing business landscape, innovation and adaptation are crucial for revenue generation. Businesses need to continuously evolve and offer new and improved products or services to stay competitive. Adapting to emerging technologies, market trends, and customer preferences can help generate revenue and stay ahead of the competition.

While these factors are important for revenue generation, it's important to note that every business is unique, and there is no one-size-fits-all approach. Revenue generation strategies may vary depending on the industry, market conditions, and specific business goals.

31

The Law of Profitability
While there is no universally recognized "Law of Profitability" in business, there are several principles and concepts that relate to profitability and guide businesses in their pursuit of financial success. Here are some key factors that contribute to profitability in business:

Revenue Generation: Increasing revenue is crucial for profitability. Businesses strive to attract customers, increase sales, and expand their market share to generate higher revenue.

Cost Management: Controlling and minimizing costs is essential for profitability. This includes optimizing operational expenses, managing supply chain costs, and reducing overhead expenditures.

Pricing Strategy: Setting the right prices for products or services is critical. Businesses need to consider factors such as market demand, competition, production costs, and customer value perception to determine optimal pricing strategies that maximize profitability.

Efficient Resource Allocation: Effectively allocating resources, such as labor, capital, and assets, ensures optimal utilization and cost efficiency, ultimately impacting profitability.

Competitive Advantage: Developing and leveraging a competitive advantage allows businesses to differentiate themselves in the market, potentially commanding higher prices and capturing a larger share of customers, leading to improved profitability.

Innovation and Adaptation: Businesses that innovate and adapt to changing market conditions can gain a competitive edge and seize new opportunities, leading to increased profitability.

Financial Management: Sound financial management practices, including effective budgeting, cash flow management, and investment decisions, are critical for maintaining profitability and long-term sustainability.

It's important to note that these factors can vary across industries and businesses, and there is no one-size-fits-all approach to profitability. Each business must assess its unique circumstances and market dynamics to develop strategies that align with its objectives and enhance profitability.

32

The Law of Return on Investment (ROI)

In the context of business, the Law of Return on Investment (ROI) is not a formal law but rather a guiding principle or concept. It suggests that businesses should evaluate and prioritize investments based on their potential return on investment. It emphasizes the importance of maximizing profitability and making sound investment decisions to achieve favorable financial outcomes.

Here are some key aspects of the Law of Return on Investment in the business context:

Investment Evaluation: Businesses should carefully assess potential investments, considering the expected return in relation to the associated costs. This evaluation helps determine whether an investment is worthwhile and aligns with the organization's goals and financial objectives.

ROI as a Performance Metric: ROI serves as a financial performance metric that helps businesses measure the efficiency and effectiveness of their investments. It enables comparison between different investment opportunities and provides insights into which investments are generating the highest returns.

Decision-Making: The Law of ROI guides decision-making processes within a business. It encourages management to allocate resources to projects or initiatives with the highest potential for generating positive returns and to prioritize investments that contribute to long-term profitability.

Risk and ROI: The Law of ROI recognizes the relationship between risk and potential returns. Investments with higher expected returns often carry higher risks, and businesses must assess and manage these risks accordingly. Balancing risk and reward is a crucial aspect of investment decision-making.

Continuous Evaluation: The Law of ROI suggests that businesses should regularly monitor and evaluate the performance of investments to ensure they are meeting expected returns. If an investment is not delivering the desired results, businesses may need to reassess their strategies and make adjustments accordingly.

While the Law of ROI is not a legal statute, it is a widely accepted principle in business and finance. By applying this concept, businesses aim to make informed decisions about resource allocation, prioritize investments, and ultimately enhance their profitability and financial success.

33

The Law of Cash Conversion Cycle
The Cash Conversion Cycle (CCC) is a financial metric that measures the time it takes for a company to convert its investments in inventory and other resources into cash flow from sales. It represents the length of time, in days, that a company's cash is tied up in its operating cycle.

The Law of Cash Conversion Cycle, on the other hand, is not a widely recognized term or concept in finance or accounting. It seems to be a phrase you have coined or encountered in a specific context. If you can provide more information or clarify the context in which you are referring to the Law of Cash Conversion Cycle.

The Cash Conversion Cycle (CCC), also known as the Operating Cycle, is a financial metric that assesses the efficiency of a company's cash flow management. It measures the time it takes for a company to convert its resources invested in inventory into cash flow from sales, and then back into cash again. The CCC is often used to evaluate the liquidity and working capital management of a business.

The CCC consists of three components:

Inventory Conversion Period: This represents the average number of days it takes for a company to convert its inventory into sales. It starts with the purchase of raw materials or finished goods and ends when the company collects cash from the sale of the inventory.

Receivables Conversion Period: This measures the average number of days it takes for a company to collect cash from its customers after a sale has been made. It includes the time taken for the customers to pay their invoices.

Payables Deferral Period: This indicates the average number of days it takes for a company to pay its suppliers for the purchases made on credit. It reflects the period in which the company can delay its payments without negatively affecting its supplier relationships.

To calculate the Cash Conversion Cycle, you subtract the payables deferral period from the sum of the inventory conversion period and the receivables conversion period:

Cash Conversion Cycle = Inventory Conversion Period + Receivables Conversion Period - Payables Deferral Period

The goal for a company is to minimize its Cash Conversion Cycle, as a shorter cycle indicates more efficient use of working capital. By reducing the time it takes to convert inventory into cash and collecting payments from customers, while extending the time to pay suppliers, a company can free up cash and improve its liquidity position.

Effective management of the Cash Conversion Cycle is crucial for businesses, as it directly impacts their cash flow, profitability, and overall financial health. By monitoring and optimizing the CCC, companies can ensure they have sufficient liquidity to meet their obligations, reduce the risk of cash flow shortages, and potentially improve their profitability.

34

The Law of Break-even Analysis

Break-even analysis is a financial tool used to determine the point at which a business or project becomes profitable or breaks even. It is based on the concept that total revenue should equal total costs in order for the business to neither make a profit nor incur a loss. The law of break-even analysis refers to the principles and calculations involved in determining the break-even point.

Here are the key components and principles of the law of break-even analysis:

Break-even point: This is the level of sales or revenue at which total costs (fixed costs and variable costs) equal total revenue. At this point, the business neither makes a profit nor suffers a loss.

Fixed costs: These are costs that remain constant regardless of the level of production or sales. Examples include rent, salaries, insurance, and equipment depreciation.

Variable costs: These costs vary directly with the level of production or sales. They include expenses such as raw materials, direct labor, and sales commissions.

Total costs: Total costs are the sum of fixed costs and variable costs. They represent the expenses incurred by the business in producing goods or services.

Total revenue: Total revenue is the amount of money generated from the sale of goods or services. It is calculated by multiplying the unit price by the quantity sold.

Contribution margin: The contribution margin is the difference between total revenue and total variable costs. It represents the amount available to cover fixed costs and contribute to profit once the break-even point is reached.

Profit and loss: If total revenue exceeds total costs, the business makes a profit. Conversely, if total costs exceed total revenue, the business incurs a loss.

The law of break-even analysis helps businesses determine the minimum level of sales or revenue required to cover costs and start generating a profit. It provides insights into the financial viability of a product, service, or business venture and assists in decision-making related to pricing, production levels, and cost management. By understanding the break-even point, businesses can assess their profitability, set sales targets, and make informed strategic choices to achieve financial success.

35

The Law of Financial Management
There isn't a specific "Law of Financial Management" that is universally recognized or defined. However, financial management encompasses a set of principles, concepts, and practices that guide the effective management of an organization's financial resources. These principles are based on sound financial principles and best practices in the field. Here are some key principles that can be considered as guiding "laws" in financial management:

Principle of profitability: Financial management aims to maximize the profitability of an organization. This involves generating revenues and managing costs in a way that leads to sustainable and long-term profitability.

Principle of risk and return: There is a direct relationship between risk and return in financial management. Higher-risk investments or strategies have the potential for higher returns, but also higher potential losses. Financial managers must carefully assess and balance the risk and return trade-off to achieve optimal results.

Principle of time value of money: This principle recognizes that the value of money changes over time due to factors such as inflation and the opportunity cost of capital. Financial management takes into account the time value of money by discounting future cash flows and making decisions based on their present value.

Principle of diversification: Diversification is a risk management strategy that involves spreading investments or resources across different assets or activities to reduce risk. Financial management encourages diversification to minimize the impact of adverse events or changes in market conditions.

Principle of liquidity: Liquidity refers to the availability of cash or easily convertible assets to meet short-term obligations. Financial management emphasizes maintaining an appropriate level of liquidity to ensure the organization's ability to meet its financial obligations and handle unexpected expenses.

Principle of leverage: Leverage refers to the use of borrowed funds to finance investments or operations. Financial management involves optimizing the use of leverage to maximize returns while managing the associated risks.

Principle of capital structure: Financial management involves determining the optimal mix of debt and equity financing to fund the organization's operations and investments. This principle considers factors such as the cost of capital, risk tolerance, and the organization's capital structure targets.

Principle of transparency and accountability: Financial management requires maintaining transparency in financial reporting and being accountable to stakeholders. This includes accurate financial reporting, compliance with regulations and accounting standards, and effective communication with investors, lenders, and other stakeholders.

While these principles provide a foundation for effective financial management, it's important to note that financial management practices can vary depending on the specific industry, organization size, and objectives. Additionally, financial management is influenced by legal and regulatory frameworks, accounting standards, and economic conditions.

36

The Law of Budgeting
The Law of Budgeting refers to the principle and process of creating and managing a budget for personal or organizational financial purposes. While not a formal law in the legal sense, it represents a fundamental principle that guides individuals, businesses, and governments in their financial planning and decision-making.

The key aspects of the Law of Budgeting include:

Planning: Budgeting begins with setting financial goals and objectives, identifying income sources, and estimating expenses. It involves projecting future financial needs and determining the resources required to meet those needs.

Allocation: Once the financial goals are defined, budgeting involves allocating available resources in a manner that aligns with those goals. This includes determining how much money should be allocated to different categories such as housing, transportation, food, savings, and debt repayment.

Prioritization: The Law of Budgeting emphasizes the importance of prioritizing expenses based on their relative importance and urgency. It requires individuals or organizations to make conscious choices about spending and to allocate resources to the most critical areas first.

Monitoring and Control: Effective budgeting involves regular monitoring of actual income and expenses to ensure they align with the planned budget. This allows for timely adjustments and course corrections if there are deviations or unexpected changes in financial circumstances.

Discipline: Budgeting requires discipline and self-control to adhere to the planned spending limits and avoid unnecessary or impulsive purchases. It involves making informed financial decisions and understanding the trade-offs between short-term desires and long-term financial stability.

Flexibility: While a budget provides a framework for financial planning, it should also allow for flexibility to adapt to changing circumstances. Life events, economic conditions, and unforeseen expenses may require adjustments to the budget to ensure it remains realistic and effective.

The Law of Budgeting helps individuals and organizations achieve financial stability, avoid excessive debt, save for future goals, and make informed financial decisions. It serves as a guiding principle for effective financial management and is essential for maintaining fiscal responsibility.

37

The Law of Capital Investment

There are several principles and theories related to capital investment that guide decision-making and economic analysis. Here are a few fundamental concepts in capital investment:

Law of Diminishing Marginal Returns: This economic principle states that as additional units of a variable input (such as capital) are added to a fixed input (such as labor), the marginal output will eventually decrease. In other words, there is a point at which the benefit gained from each additional unit of capital invested diminishes.

Time Value of Money: This principle recognizes that a dollar received in the future is worth less than a dollar received today due to the opportunity cost of waiting. In capital investment, this concept is crucial in evaluating the present value of future cash flows and determining the profitability of investment projects.

Risk-Return Tradeoff: Capital investment involves taking risks, and the potential return on an investment is often related to the level of risk involved. Generally, higher-risk investments are expected to yield higher returns, while lower-risk investments have lower potential returns. This principle helps investors and businesses assess the appropriate balance between risk and reward.

Net Present Value (NPV): NPV is a financial metric used to evaluate investment opportunities. It calculates the present value of expected cash inflows and outflows associated with an investment, accounting for the time value of money. A positive NPV indicates that the investment is expected to generate more value than the initial capital invested, while a negative NPV suggests the opposite.

Internal Rate of Return (IRR): The IRR is another financial metric used to assess the profitability of an investment. It represents the discount rate at which the NPV of an investment becomes zero. If the IRR is greater than the required rate of return or cost of capital, the investment is generally considered viable.

These principles, among others, form the foundation for analyzing and making decisions regarding capital investment. While there isn't a single "Law of Capital Investment," these concepts are widely used and recognized in the field of finance and economics.

38

The Law of Debt Management
There isn't a specific "Law of Debt Management," but there are several principles and practices that guide debt management strategies. Here are some key concepts related to debt management:

Budgeting: Budgeting is a fundamental principle of debt management. It involves creating a detailed plan for income and expenses to ensure that debt obligations can be met. A well-structured budget helps individuals and organizations allocate funds for debt repayment while also covering essential expenses and saving for future needs.

Debt-to-Income Ratio: The debt-to-income ratio is a financial metric that compares an individual's or organization's total debt obligations to their income. It is a measure of the ability to manage and service debt. Lenders often use this ratio to assess creditworthiness, and individuals use it to determine their own debt capacity and affordability.

Interest Rates: Interest rates play a crucial role in debt management. Higher interest rates increase the cost of borrowing and can make it more challenging to repay debt. Managing debt involves seeking favorable interest rates, refinancing existing debt at lower rates if possible, and considering the impact of interest rates on debt affordability.

Debt Repayment Strategies: There are various strategies for repaying debt, such as the snowball method and the avalanche method. The snowball method involves paying off debts from smallest to largest, regardless of interest rates, while the avalanche method prioritizes paying off debts with the highest interest rates first. Each strategy has its advantages and may suit different individuals' financial situations.

Communication with Creditors: Open and transparent communication with creditors is important in debt management. If facing difficulties in repaying debt, individuals or organizations can reach out to creditors to discuss alternative payment arrangements, negotiate interest rates, or explore debt consolidation options. Communication can help find solutions that work for both parties and prevent further financial challenges.

Credit Score Management: Maintaining a good credit score is essential for effective debt management. A high credit score can lead to better borrowing terms, lower interest rates, and more favorable credit opportunities. Managing debt responsibly, making timely payments, and keeping credit utilization low are some ways to maintain a healthy credit score.

While there isn't a specific law governing debt management, these principles and practices are commonly employed to effectively manage and repay debt. It's important to seek advice from financial professionals or credit counseling services to develop a personalized debt management plan based on individual circumstances.

39

The Law of Risk Management
There are various principles and frameworks that guide risk management practices. Risk management is the process of identifying, assessing, and mitigating risks to minimize potential negative impacts and optimize opportunities. Here are some key concepts related to risk management:

Risk Assessment: Risk assessment involves identifying and evaluating potential risks and their potential consequences. This step includes analyzing the likelihood of risks occurring and assessing their potential impact on objectives or outcomes. Various techniques such as risk registers, risk matrices, and scenario analysis can be used to assess risks.

Risk Identification: Risk identification involves systematically identifying and documenting potential risks that could affect an organization, project, or individual. This process typically involves engaging stakeholders, conducting risk workshops, reviewing historical data, and considering various sources of risk.

Risk Mitigation: Once risks are identified, risk mitigation strategies are developed to reduce the likelihood or impact of those risks. This may involve implementing controls, developing contingency plans, transferring risk through insurance, or taking other actions to manage risks effectively.

Risk Monitoring and Review: Risk management is an ongoing process, and risks should be continually monitored and reviewed. Regular monitoring ensures that risks are effectively managed and that new risks are identified and addressed promptly. This step involves tracking risk indicators, reviewing risk treatment plans, and adjusting risk management strategies as needed.

Risk Appetite and Tolerance: Risk appetite refers to the amount of risk an organization or individual is willing to accept to achieve their objectives. Risk tolerance is the level of risk that can be tolerated within that appetite. Establishing clear risk appetite and tolerance levels helps guide decision-making and risk management efforts.

Risk Communication: Effective risk management involves transparent and timely communication of risks and their potential impacts. Stakeholders need to be informed about risks, mitigation strategies, and progress in managing risks. Clear communication facilitates understanding, collaboration, and informed decision-making.

Risk Culture: Developing a risk-aware culture within an organization is important for effective risk management. This involves fostering a mindset where individuals understand the importance of risk management, take ownership of risk responsibilities, and proactively identify and address risks.

While not a specific law, these principles and practices form the foundation of risk management. Organizations and individuals often adopt established frameworks such as ISO 31000, COSO ERM, or PMI's Risk Management Framework to guide their risk management efforts.

40

The Law of Crisis Management
Crisis management is a discipline that involves preparing for, responding to, and recovering from unexpected events or crises. While not a law, there are key principles and practices that guide effective crisis management. Here are some important concepts related to crisis management:

Preparedness: Crisis preparedness involves proactively identifying potential risks and developing plans and protocols to respond to them. This includes creating a crisis management team, establishing communication channels, conducting risk assessments, and developing response strategies. Preparedness also involves training and educating stakeholders on crisis management procedures.

Crisis Response: When a crisis occurs, an effective response is crucial. This involves activating the crisis management team, implementing pre-defined response plans, and executing coordinated actions to mitigate the impact of the crisis. Clear roles, responsibilities, and decision-making processes should be established to ensure a swift and effective response.

Communication: Effective communication is paramount during a crisis. Timely and accurate information must be disseminated to stakeholders, including employees, customers, partners, and the public. Transparent and consistent communication helps manage expectations, address concerns, and maintain trust and credibility. Crisis communication plans should be developed in advance to guide communication efforts.

Adaptive Decision-Making: Crisis situations are often dynamic and rapidly evolving. Effective crisis management requires adaptive decision-making to respond to changing circumstances. This involves gathering real-time information, assessing the situation, and making decisions based on the best available data. Agility and flexibility are crucial to adjust strategies and actions as needed.

Collaboration and Coordination: Crisis management often involves multiple stakeholders and organizations. Collaborative efforts and coordination among various parties, such as government agencies, emergency services, and other relevant entities, are essential. Establishing effective partnerships and coordination mechanisms in advance helps streamline crisis response and maximize resources.

Learning and Evaluation: After a crisis has been resolved, it is important to conduct a thorough evaluation and learn from the experience. This includes analyzing the effectiveness of response efforts, identifying areas for improvement, and updating crisis management plans accordingly. Continuous learning and improvement help organizations enhance their crisis management capabilities.

While there isn't a specific law governing crisis management, these principles and practices are widely recognized as best practices in the field. Organizations often develop their own crisis management frameworks or adopt established models like the Incident Command System (ICS) or the National Incident Management System (NIMS) to guide their crisis management efforts.

41

The Law of Customer Relationship Management (CRM)

Customer relationship management is a strategic approach that organizations use to manage their interactions and relationships with customers. While not a law, there are key principles and practices that guide effective CRM. Here are some important concepts related to CRM:

Customer-Centric Approach: CRM emphasizes putting the customer at the center of business activities. It involves understanding customer needs, preferences, and behaviors to deliver personalized experiences and build strong relationships. Organizations need to prioritize customer satisfaction and tailor their products, services, and interactions accordingly.

Customer Data Management: Effective CRM relies on capturing and managing customer data. This includes gathering information about customers' demographics, preferences, purchase history, and interactions with the organization. Robust data management systems and processes are essential to ensure data accuracy, security, and accessibility for informed decision-making and targeted marketing efforts.

Customer Segmentation: Customers have different characteristics, behaviors, and needs. CRM involves segmenting customers into distinct groups based on these factors. This segmentation helps organizations better understand their customer base, develop targeted marketing strategies, and deliver personalized experiences to different customer segments.

Relationship Building: CRM focuses on building and nurturing long-term relationships with customers. This involves engaging with customers at various touchpoints, providing exceptional customer service, and maintaining open lines of communication. Building trust, loyalty, and customer advocacy are key objectives of CRM.

Multichannel Integration: Customers interact with organizations through multiple channels, including websites, social media, phone calls, and in-person interactions. CRM aims to integrate these channels to ensure a consistent and seamless customer experience across all touchpoints. Organizations should strive to provide a unified view of customer interactions and enable customers to switch between channels effortlessly.

Customer Analytics: CRM leverages customer data and analytics to gain insights into customer behavior, preferences, and trends. Analyzing customer data helps organizations make data-driven decisions, identify opportunities for growth, and measure the effectiveness of marketing and sales efforts. Predictive analytics can also be used to anticipate customer needs and tailor offerings accordingly.

Continuous Improvement: CRM is an ongoing process of continuous improvement. Organizations should regularly evaluate their CRM strategies, monitor customer satisfaction and feedback, and make necessary adjustments to enhance customer relationships. This includes identifying and addressing pain points, implementing customer feedback loops, and staying updated with evolving customer expectations and market trends.

While there isn't a specific law governing CRM, these principles and practices form the foundation of effective customer relationship management. Organizations often adopt CRM systems and strategies to support their CRM efforts, integrating technology and processes to manage and optimize customer interactions and relationships.

42

The Law of Customer Retention
The Law of Customer Retention refers to the principle that retaining existing customers is generally more cost-effective and valuable than acquiring new customers. It recognizes the importance of building long-term relationships with customers and emphasizes the need for businesses to focus on customer retention strategies.

Here are some key aspects and principles related to the Law of Customer Retention:

Customer Lifetime Value (CLTV): CLTV represents the total value a customer brings to a business over their entire relationship. By understanding the CLTV, businesses can evaluate the financial impact of customer retention and make informed decisions about resource allocation.

Customer Churn: Churn refers to the rate at which customers stop doing business with a company. High churn rates can be detrimental to a business, as it signifies lost revenue and the need to constantly acquire new customers. By reducing churn through effective customer retention efforts, businesses can enhance their profitability.

Customer Satisfaction: Ensuring customer satisfaction is crucial for customer retention. Satisfied customers are more likely to remain loyal and continue their relationship with a business. Providing high-quality products, exceptional customer service, and addressing customer concerns are vital elements in maintaining satisfaction levels.

Relationship Building: Building strong relationships with customers is a cornerstone of customer retention. This involves engaging with customers beyond the initial sale, understanding their needs and preferences, and personalizing the customer experience. Effective communication and regular interactions help foster loyalty and strengthen the bond between the customer and the business.

Loyalty Programs: Loyalty programs are designed to reward and incentivize customers for their continued patronage. These programs can include discounts, exclusive offers, personalized recommendations, or a points-based system that leads to future rewards. Loyalty programs can significantly contribute to customer retention by providing value and encouraging repeat purchases.

Proactive Customer Service: Proactively addressing customer needs and resolving issues promptly is essential for customer retention. By being responsive, attentive, and helpful, businesses can demonstrate their commitment to customer satisfaction. Anticipating customer concerns and providing proactive solutions can prevent problems and further strengthen the customer-business relationship.

Continuous Improvement: Regularly seeking feedback from customers and using it to improve products, services, and overall customer experience is critical for customer retention. By actively listening to customers, adapting to their evolving needs, and striving for continuous improvement, businesses can maintain their relevance and competitive edge.

Remember, the Law of Customer Retention emphasizes that businesses should prioritize retaining existing customers alongside acquiring new ones. By focusing on customer satisfaction, relationship building, and proactive customer service, businesses can foster loyalty, reduce churn, and ultimately drive long-term success.

43

The Law of Customer Loyalty
The Law of Customer Loyalty is a concept that emphasizes the importance of building strong relationships with customers in order to foster their loyalty and increase business success. It recognizes that loyal customers are more likely to make repeat purchases, spend more money, and recommend a company or brand to others. The Law of Customer Loyalty can be summarized by the following key principles:

Customer Satisfaction: Providing a positive and satisfying customer experience is crucial for building loyalty. Meeting or exceeding customer expectations in terms of product quality, service, and support is essential.

Relationship Building: Building strong relationships with customers is fundamental to fostering loyalty. This involves understanding their needs, preferences, and expectations, and engaging with them in a personalized and meaningful way.

Consistency: Consistency in delivering high-quality products, services, and experiences is essential for building trust and loyalty. Customers should have confidence that their experience will be consistently positive each time they interact with a company or brand.

Communication and Engagement: Effective communication and engagement with customers help to create a sense of connection and loyalty. Keeping customers informed about new products, promotions, and updates, as well as actively seeking their feedback, demonstrates that their opinions are valued.

Reward and Recognition: Recognizing and rewarding loyal customers can further strengthen their loyalty. Loyalty programs, exclusive offers, discounts, and personalized incentives can incentivize customers to continue their relationship with a brand.

Customer Retention: Retaining existing customers is more cost-effective than acquiring new ones. The Law of Customer Loyalty emphasizes the importance of implementing strategies and initiatives to retain and nurture existing customer relationships.

Continuous Improvement: Constantly striving to improve products, services, and customer experiences is vital for maintaining customer loyalty. Companies should proactively seek feedback, identify areas for improvement, and take action to enhance customer satisfaction.

By adhering to the principles of the Law of Customer Loyalty, businesses can cultivate strong customer relationships, enhance customer satisfaction, and foster long-term loyalty, which ultimately leads to increased profitability and sustainable growth.

44

The Law of Market Segmentation

The concept of the Law of Market Segmentation revolves around the idea that markets are composed of diverse groups of individuals or organizations with distinct needs, preferences, and characteristics. It emphasizes the importance of understanding and dividing the market into meaningful segments to effectively target and serve customers. The Law of Market Segmentation encompasses several key principles:

Customer Heterogeneity: Recognizing that customers within a market are not uniform and exhibit variations in their preferences, behaviors, and demographics. Market segmentation acknowledges this diversity and seeks to identify and understand these differences.

Segmentation Variables: Identifying and utilizing relevant segmentation variables to divide the market into distinct groups. Segmentation variables can include demographic factors (age, gender, income), psychographic factors (lifestyle, values, attitudes), geographic location, and behavioral patterns (purchasing behavior, product usage).

Targeting: Once market segments are identified, selecting the most attractive and viable segments to target. This involves evaluating the size, growth potential, profitability, and accessibility of each segment and determining which segments align best with the company's resources and capabilities.

Customization: Tailoring marketing strategies, products, and services to meet the specific needs and preferences of each segment. This involves developing targeted messaging, positioning, and value propositions that resonate with the unique characteristics and requirements of the segment.

Differentiation: Differentiating the company or brand from competitors within each segment by offering unique benefits, features, or experiences. This can involve product differentiation, pricing strategies, distribution channels, or promotional tactics that set the company apart and create a competitive advantage.

Marketing Mix Adaptation: Adjusting the marketing mix (product, price, place, promotion) for each segment to maximize appeal and effectiveness. Recognizing that different segments may have varying needs and preferences, marketers must adapt their strategies accordingly to ensure relevance and resonance.

Continuous Evaluation: Regularly assessing market segments, monitoring changes in customer behavior, preferences, and market dynamics. Markets are dynamic, and customer needs evolve over time. Therefore, it is crucial to continually review and update segmentation strategies to maintain relevance and effectiveness.

By following the principles of the Law of Market Segmentation, companies can better understand their customers, tailor their offerings, and allocate resources more efficiently. This approach enables businesses to focus their efforts on the most promising market segments, develop targeted marketing campaigns, and ultimately achieve higher customer satisfaction, market share, and profitability.

45

The Law of Targeting

The Law of Targeting refers to the practice of identifying and focusing on a specific target market or audience with the aim of maximizing marketing effectiveness and efficiency. It emphasizes the importance of directing marketing efforts towards a well-defined group of individuals or organizations who are most likely to be interested in and responsive to the company's products or services. The Law of Targeting encompasses the following key principles:

Market Analysis: Conducting thorough market research and analysis to gain insights into the characteristics, needs, and preferences of potential customers. This involves examining demographic, psychographic, geographic, and behavioral data to identify the most attractive target segments.

Target Market Selection: Choosing the most suitable target market(s) based on the analysis. This decision is influenced by factors such as market size, growth potential, competition, and alignment with the company's capabilities and resources.

Segmentation: Dividing the overall market into distinct segments based on shared characteristics and preferences. This helps to identify the specific groups within the target market that are most likely to respond favorably to the company's offerings.

Target Audience Identification: Within the selected target market segment(s), identifying the specific individuals or organizations that the company will direct its marketing efforts towards. This involves creating customer profiles or buyer personas that represent the ideal customers for the company.

Positioning: Developing a clear and differentiated brand positioning that resonates with the target audience. This involves communicating the unique value proposition and benefits of the company's products or services in a way that appeals to the target market.

Marketing Strategy Alignment: Aligning marketing strategies, tactics, and messages with the needs, preferences, and behaviors of the target audience. This includes selecting appropriate marketing channels, crafting targeted messaging, and designing marketing campaigns that effectively reach and engage the target market.

Measurement and Optimization: Continuously monitoring and measuring the effectiveness of marketing efforts targeted at the chosen audience. This involves tracking key performance indicators (KPIs), analyzing customer feedback, and making data-driven adjustments to optimize targeting strategies and improve overall marketing outcomes.

By adhering to the principles of the Law of Targeting, companies can focus their marketing resources on the most relevant and receptive audience, leading to more efficient resource allocation, increased customer engagement, higher conversion rates, and ultimately, greater business success.

46

The Law of Customer Acquisition

The "Law of Customer Acquisition" is not a well-known or widely recognized term or concept in the field of marketing or business. It may be a term specific to a certain individual, organization, or industry. However, I can provide you with general information about customer acquisition in the context of marketing.

Customer acquisition refers to the process of attracting and converting potential customers into paying customers for a product or service. It involves various marketing strategies and tactics aimed at creating awareness, generating interest, and ultimately convincing prospects to make a purchase.

Here are some key aspects of customer acquisition:

Targeting: Identifying and understanding the target audience for your product or service. This involves creating buyer personas and conducting market research to determine the characteristics, needs, and preferences of potential customers.

Marketing Channels: Selecting the appropriate marketing channels to reach and engage with your target audience. This can include digital channels like search engine marketing, social media advertising, email marketing, content marketing, as well as traditional channels such as television, radio, and print.

Lead Generation: Generating leads or inquiries from potential customers who have shown interest in your product or service. This can be done through various methods such as online forms, landing pages, lead magnets, events, or referrals.

Conversion: Convincing leads to become paying customers. This involves nurturing the relationship with leads through effective communication, providing valuable information, addressing their concerns, and guiding them through the buying process.

Measurement and Optimization: Tracking and analyzing the effectiveness of your customer acquisition efforts. This includes monitoring key metrics such as conversion rates, customer acquisition costs, return on investment (ROI), and making adjustments to optimize your marketing strategies accordingly.

While the term "Law of Customer Acquisition" may not have a specific definition, these principles and strategies form the foundation of customer acquisition in marketing. It's important to note that customer acquisition is just one part of the broader customer lifecycle, which also includes customer retention and customer loyalty.

47

The Law of Market Research

The term "Law of Market Research" is not a widely recognized or commonly used term. However, market research is a fundamental practice in the field of business and marketing. It involves gathering and analyzing information about the target market, customers, competitors, and other relevant factors to make informed business decisions. While there may not be a specific "law" associated with market research, I can provide you with an overview of the key principles and processes involved.

Purpose and Objectives: Clearly defining the purpose and objectives of the market research. This could include understanding customer needs and preferences, assessing market trends, evaluating the potential demand for a product or service, identifying target segments, or gauging customer satisfaction.

Research Design: Planning and designing the research study, including selecting the appropriate research methods and tools. This could involve primary research (collecting new data through surveys, interviews, observations) or secondary research (analyzing existing data and information from various sources).

Data Collection: Gathering relevant data from the target market or audience. This could be done through surveys, focus groups, interviews, observations, online research, or other data collection techniques.

Data Analysis: Analyzing and interpreting the collected data to derive meaningful insights. This could involve quantitative analysis (statistical techniques, data modeling) or qualitative analysis (thematic analysis, coding of responses).

Insights and Recommendations: Drawing conclusions and actionable recommendations based on the research findings. This could involve identifying market opportunities, refining marketing strategies, developing new products or services, or making informed business decisions.

Continuous Research: Recognizing that market research is an ongoing process, and regularly updating and refining the research efforts as market conditions, customer preferences, or competitive landscapes change over time.

Market research helps organizations gain a deeper understanding of their target market, make informed business decisions, and develop effective marketing strategies. It provides insights into customer behavior, market trends, competitive positioning, and helps minimize risks associated with launching new products or entering new markets.

While there is no specific "law" associated with market research, it is a critical component of any successful business and plays a key role in driving strategic decision-making and business growth.

48

The Law of Competitive Analysis

The Law of Competitive Analysis is a concept that refers to the practice of evaluating and analyzing the competitive landscape within a specific industry or market. It is an essential component of strategic planning and business decision-making. The Law of Competitive Analysis helps businesses understand their position in relation to their competitors, identify potential threats and opportunities, and develop effective strategies to gain a competitive advantage.

Here are some key principles associated with the Law of Competitive Analysis:

Know your competitors: Businesses need to identify and understand their competitors, including both direct and indirect competitors. This involves researching and analyzing their products, services, pricing, distribution channels, marketing strategies, strengths, weaknesses, and market share.

Analyze the competitive landscape: It is important to assess the overall competitive landscape to determine the intensity of competition, the key players, and any potential new entrants or disruptive forces. This analysis can be done through market research, industry reports, and monitoring industry trends.

Identify competitive advantages and disadvantages: By analyzing competitors, businesses can identify their own competitive advantages and disadvantages. This involves understanding what sets them apart from their competitors, such as unique features, superior quality, cost leadership, or strong brand recognition. It also helps identify areas where the business may be at a disadvantage and needs to improve.

SWOT analysis: A SWOT analysis (Strengths, Weaknesses, Opportunities, and Threats) is a common tool used in competitive analysis. It helps businesses evaluate their internal strengths and weaknesses and external opportunities and threats. By understanding these factors, businesses can develop strategies to capitalize on strengths, minimize weaknesses, seize opportunities, and mitigate threats.

Continuous monitoring and adaptation: Competitive analysis is not a one-time activity but an ongoing process. The business environment is dynamic, and competitors can change their strategies or introduce new products/services. Therefore, it is crucial to continuously monitor the competitive landscape and adapt strategies accordingly.

Ethical considerations: While conducting competitive analysis, it is important for businesses to adhere to ethical guidelines and legal requirements. They should gather information from publicly available sources and avoid engaging in unethical practices, such as industrial espionage or unauthorized access to confidential information.

The Law of Competitive Analysis emphasizes the significance of understanding the competitive landscape to make informed business decisions. By gaining insights into competitors' strengths, weaknesses, and strategies, businesses can position themselves effectively and develop strategies to stay competitive and succeed in their industry or market.

49

The Law of Product Development

There are various principles and best practices that can guide the process of product development. These principles are based on industry knowledge and experience and can help organizations effectively create and launch successful products. Here are some key considerations in product development:

Customer-centric approach: Product development should be driven by a deep understanding of customer needs and preferences. Conducting market research, gathering customer feedback, and incorporating user-centered design principles are essential for developing products that meet customer expectations.

Clear objectives and requirements: Clearly define the objectives and requirements for the product. This includes identifying the target market, specifying product features and functionalities, setting performance standards, and establishing project timelines and budgets.

Iterative development process: Product development often involves an iterative process, with multiple stages and feedback loops. This allows for continuous improvement and refinement of the product based on user feedback and market insights. Agile development methodologies, such as Scrum or Kanban, can be useful in managing iterative product development processes.

Cross-functional collaboration: Successful product development requires collaboration and coordination among various teams and departments, including engineering, design, marketing, and sales. Foster a culture of collaboration and ensure effective communication to align everyone's efforts toward a common goal.

Risk assessment and mitigation: Identify and assess potential risks and challenges that could impact the product development process. This includes technological risks, market uncertainties, regulatory compliance, and resource constraints. Develop contingency plans and mitigation strategies to address these risks proactively.

Testing and validation: Rigorous testing and validation are crucial to ensure the quality and reliability of the product. Conduct prototype testing, user testing, and performance testing to validate the product's functionality, usability, and performance. Iterate based on feedback and refine the product accordingly.

Scalability and adaptability: Consider the scalability and adaptability of the product. Anticipate future growth and market trends, and design the product in a way that allows for easy scalability and flexibility to accommodate evolving customer needs and technological advancements.

Continuous improvement: Product development doesn't end with the product launch. Monitor customer feedback, track product performance, and gather market intelligence to identify areas for improvement and future product enhancements. Regularly update and innovate the product to stay competitive and meet evolving market demands.

While there may not be a specific "Law of Product Development," following these principles can help organizations navigate the complex process of developing successful products. Each industry and organization may have its own unique considerations and challenges, so it's important to tailor these principles to specific contexts and adapt them as needed.

50

The Law of Product Life Cycle

The Product Life Cycle (PLC) is a concept that describes the stages a product goes through from its introduction to its eventual decline in the market. It is a widely recognized marketing theory that helps businesses understand and manage the dynamics of their products over time. The PLC consists of four main stages: introduction, growth, maturity, and decline. However, it is important to note that not all products follow this exact pattern, and the duration of each stage can vary significantly depending on various factors.

This is the initial stage when a new product is introduced into the market. It is characterized by low sales and little to no profit due to limited consumer awareness and a small customer base. Companies typically invest heavily in marketing and product promotion during this stage to create product awareness and attract early adopters. Prices may be relatively high to recoup development costs.

Growth: In the growth stage, sales and profits start to increase significantly. Consumer awareness and demand for the product grow, leading to a larger market share. Competitors may enter the market, leading to increased competition. Companies focus on expanding their customer base, improving product quality, and enhancing distribution channels. Prices may start to decrease as economies of scale are achieved.

Maturity: The maturity stage is characterized by a stable market with high levels of competition. Sales growth slows down as the product reaches its peak market penetration. The customer base is relatively large, and most potential customers have already adopted the product. Companies often focus on maintaining market share, improving customer loyalty, and introducing product variations or extensions. Price competition becomes more intense during this stage.

Decline: In the decline stage, sales and profits start to decline. This can happen due to various reasons, such as changing consumer preferences, technological advancements, or the emergence of substitute products. Companies may choose to discontinue the product or reduce marketing efforts and focus on more profitable products. Prices may be reduced further to sell off remaining inventory.

It's important to note that not all products follow the same trajectory, and the length of each stage can vary. Additionally, companies can employ strategies such as product innovation, repositioning, or targeting new markets to extend the life cycle of their products or even revive declining products.

Understanding the product life cycle is crucial for businesses as it helps them make informed decisions regarding product development, marketing strategies, pricing, and resource allocation throughout the different stages of a product's life.

51

The Law of Product-Market Fit

The Law of Product-Market Fit is a concept that relates to the success of a product or service in the market. It states that a company's product or service must satisfy a strong market demand and meet the needs of its target customers in order to achieve significant success and sustainable growth.

The term "product-market fit" was coined by Marc Andreessen, a prominent venture capitalist and co-founder of Andreessen Horowitz. According to Andreessen, achieving product-market fit is the most important factor for a startup's success. He defines product-market fit as being in a good market with a product that can satisfy that market.

When a product or service achieves product-market fit, it means that there is a strong alignment between what the product offers and what the market wants. It indicates that the product addresses a genuine need or pain point of customers and provides a solution that is superior to existing alternatives. This fit results in a significant demand for the product, positive customer feedback, and sustainable growth for the company.

Product-market fit is crucial because it validates the viability and potential success of a business. It helps attract customers, generate revenue, and build a loyal user base. Without product-market fit, a company may struggle to gain traction, face low demand, or fail to differentiate itself from competitors.

Achieving product-market fit often requires a deep understanding of the target market, including customer preferences, pain points, and behaviors. It involves continuous iteration, feedback collection, and refinement of the product based on customer insights. Companies may need to make adjustments to their product features, pricing, marketing strategies, or even pivot their business model to better align with the market.

In summary, the Law of Product-Market Fit emphasizes the importance of finding a strong fit between a product or service and the needs of the market. By achieving product-market fit, a company can establish a strong foundation for long-term success and growth.

52

The Law of Intellectual Property

The Law of Intellectual Property refers to the legal framework that governs the protection and enforcement of various forms of intellectual creations or intangible assets. It encompasses a range of legal principles, statutes, and regulations designed to safeguard the rights of creators, innovators, and owners of intellectual property.

Intellectual property (IP) refers to intangible assets that are the result of human creativity and intellectual effort. It includes inventions, trademarks, copyrights, trade secrets, and industrial designs. The primary objective of intellectual property laws is to provide exclusive rights and incentives to creators and innovators, encouraging them to invest time, resources, and effort into the development of new ideas and creations.

The key components of intellectual property law include:

Patents: Patents grant exclusive rights to inventors for new and useful inventions, providing them with a limited monopoly to exploit their inventions commercially. Patent protection typically involves disclosing the invention in a detailed patent application and satisfying the legal requirements for novelty, non-obviousness, and industrial applicability.

Trademarks: Trademarks protect distinctive signs, symbols, logos, names, or phrases used to identify and distinguish goods or services of one business from those of others. Trademark registration grants the owner exclusive rights to use the mark and prevent others from using similar marks that may cause confusion among consumers.

Copyright: Copyright protects original works of authorship, including literary, artistic, musical, and dramatic works. It gives the creator exclusive rights to reproduce, distribute, display, perform, and modify their work. Copyright protection arises automatically upon the creation of the work, but formal registration can provide additional benefits and legal advantages.

Trade Secrets: Trade secrets encompass confidential and proprietary information that provides a competitive advantage to a business. It can include formulas, manufacturing processes, customer lists, marketing strategies, and other confidential business information. Unlike patents or copyrights, trade secrets rely on maintaining secrecy and implementing measures to protect against unauthorized disclosure or use.

Intellectual property laws vary across jurisdictions, but they generally serve common purposes, including:

Encouraging innovation and creativity by providing legal protection and incentives.
Facilitating the commercialization and exploitation of intellectual property.
Balancing the rights of creators and innovators with the public interest.
Promoting fair competition and preventing unauthorized use or infringement.

Establishing mechanisms for resolving disputes and enforcing IP rights.

Enforcement of intellectual property rights typically involves legal actions, such as civil litigation or administrative procedures, to seek remedies for infringement, including damages, injunctions, or other forms of relief. International agreements and treaties, such as the World Intellectual Property Organization (WIPO) and the Agreement on Trade-Related Aspects of Intellectual Property Rights (TRIPS), provide a framework for harmonizing intellectual property laws globally and facilitating international cooperation and protection.

Overall, the Law of Intellectual Property plays a vital role in promoting innovation, creativity, and economic development by protecting and rewarding the valuable intangible assets generated by individuals, businesses, and society as a whole.

53

The Law of Patents

The Law of Patents has significant implications for businesses. Patents provide exclusive rights to inventors or businesses, allowing them to protect their inventions or innovative processes from unauthorized use by others. Here are some key ways in which the Law of Patents impacts businesses:

Protection of Intellectual Property: Patents enable businesses to safeguard their intellectual property and prevent competitors from copying or exploiting their inventions. By securing patent protection, businesses can establish a competitive advantage, maintain market exclusivity, and defend their innovations from infringement.

Incentives for Innovation: The Law of Patents incentivizes businesses to invest in research and development (R&D) activities to create new and inventive products, technologies, or processes. The exclusivity provided by patents encourages businesses to allocate resources and take risks in developing innovative solutions, knowing that they can protect and profit from their inventions.

Market Differentiation and Branding: Patents can help businesses differentiate themselves in the marketplace. By patenting unique and inventive technologies or products, businesses can establish a distinct brand identity and position themselves as industry leaders. Patents can also enhance the value and reputation of a business, attracting customers and investors who recognize the innovative nature of its offerings.

Revenue Generation and Licensing: Patents can serve as valuable assets for businesses. Patented inventions can be licensed or sold to other businesses, generating revenue through royalties or outright sales. Licensing agreements allow businesses to monetize their intellectual property while leveraging the expertise and resources of other companies for commercialization and distribution.

Market Exclusivity and Market Entry Barriers: Patents grant businesses a period of exclusivity, during which they can prevent competitors from entering the market with similar products or technologies. This exclusivity can provide businesses with a head start, allowing them to capture market share, establish customer loyalty, and recoup R&D investments before competitors can enter the market.

Defense against Infringement: Patents enable businesses to enforce their rights and take legal action against parties that infringe upon their patented inventions. This can involve litigation, seeking injunctions, and pursuing damages or royalties from infringers. Patents serve as a deterrent against potential infringers and provide a legal basis for resolving disputes.

Collaborative Opportunities: Patents can facilitate collaborations and partnerships between businesses. By licensing or cross-licensing patents, businesses can access each other's intellectual property, fostering innovation, and advancing technological progress collectively.

It's worth noting that navigating the complexities of patent law can be challenging, requiring expertise in intellectual property and legal considerations. Businesses often seek the advice of patent attorneys or intellectual property professionals to ensure proper understanding, protection, and enforcement of their patent rights.

In summary, the Law of Patents plays a critical role in shaping business strategies and outcomes. It encourages innovation, protects intellectual property, promotes competitiveness, and provides businesses with opportunities for growth, market differentiation, revenue generation, and collaboration.

54

The Law of Copyrights

The Law of Copyrights has significant implications for businesses, particularly in relation to the creation, use, and protection of creative works. Here are some key considerations regarding the Law of Copyrights in the business context:

Protection of Business Assets: Copyright law enables businesses to protect their original creative works, such as software code, website content, marketing materials, product designs, and other artistic or literary works. By obtaining copyright protection, businesses can prevent others from copying or using their works without authorization, safeguarding their valuable intellectual property assets.

Ownership and Licensing: Businesses must be aware of copyright ownership and licensing issues. In many jurisdictions, when employees create copyrightable works within the scope of their employment, the employer automatically becomes the owner of the copyrights. However, it is crucial to establish clear agreements, such as employment contracts or work-for-hire agreements, to explicitly address copyright ownership. Additionally, businesses often engage in licensing agreements to grant or obtain permission to use copyrighted works owned by others.

Infringement Risk Mitigation: Understanding copyright law helps businesses mitigate the risk of inadvertently infringing on the copyrights of others. It is essential to conduct due diligence and ensure that the use of third-party copyrighted material, such as images, music, or text, is done with appropriate permissions or falls within the scope of fair use or other applicable exceptions.

Original Content Creation: Copyright law encourages businesses to create original content and materials to differentiate themselves in the marketplace. By developing unique and creative works, businesses can establish their brand identity, attract customers, and gain a competitive advantage. Copyright protection ensures that the business's original works are not copied or used by competitors without permission.

Digital Content and Online Presence: In the digital era, businesses must navigate copyright law in the context of online content creation and distribution. This includes considerations such as the use of copyrighted materials in websites, social media posts, digital marketing campaigns, and online publishing. It is important for businesses to understand the rules and limitations surrounding the use of copyrighted works in digital environments and ensure compliance with copyright laws and platform-specific guidelines.

Copyright Infringement Claims and Disputes: Businesses should be prepared to address copyright infringement claims or disputes involving their copyrighted works. This may involve initiating legal action against infringers or defending against allegations of infringement. It is advisable to work with legal professionals experienced in copyright law to handle such situations effectively and protect the business's rights and interests.

Copyright Education and Compliance: Businesses can benefit from educating their employees about copyright law and implementing internal policies and guidelines to ensure compliance. This can include providing training on copyright awareness, establishing procedures for obtaining necessary permissions or licenses, and implementing digital asset management systems to track copyrighted works and usage permissions.

It is important for businesses to consult with legal professionals specializing in copyright law to ensure that their practices align with applicable regulations and to protect their own copyrighted works while respecting the rights of others. By understanding and adhering to the Law of Copyrights, businesses can mitigate legal risks, protect their intellectual property assets, and leverage creativity to drive success and competitive advantage.

55

The Law of Trademarks
The Law of Trademarks refers to the legal framework that governs the protection and enforcement of trademarks. Trademarks are distinctive signs, symbols, logos, names, or phrases used to identify and distinguish the goods or services of one business from those of others.

Here are key aspects of the Law of Trademarks:

Identifying and Distinguishing Goods or Services: Trademarks serve as identifiers of the source or origin of goods or services. They help consumers recognize and distinguish the products or services of one business from those of others in the marketplace. Trademarks can take various forms, including word marks, logos, slogans, or even distinctive packaging.

Exclusive Rights: Trademark law grants exclusive rights to the owner of a registered trademark, allowing them to use the mark in connection with their goods or services and to prevent others from using similar marks that may cause confusion among consumers. The owner of a registered trademark can take legal action against infringers and seek remedies such as injunctions, damages, or the cessation of infringing activities.

Trademark Registration: While trademark rights can be acquired through use in commerce, registration of a trademark with the appropriate trademark office provides additional legal benefits and protection. Registering a trademark strengthens the rights of the owner, establishes a public record of ownership, and provides nationwide or international protection (depending on the jurisdiction) against unauthorized use or infringement.

Distinctiveness and Non-generic Use: Trademarks must possess distinctiveness, meaning they should be sufficiently unique and recognizable to identify the goods or services of a particular business. Generic or descriptive terms that do not distinguish the goods or services from others cannot function as trademarks. However, trademarks can acquire distinctiveness over time through continuous use and consumer recognition.

Trademark Infringement: Trademark infringement occurs when someone uses a trademark that is confusingly similar to a registered trademark or one that may cause confusion among consumers regarding the source of goods or services. Infringement may involve using a similar mark, imitating a trademark, or using a registered trademark without permission. Trademark owners can take legal action to protect their rights and seek remedies against infringers.

Trademark Licensing and Assignments: Trademark owners can license or assign their trademark rights to other parties. Licensing allows third parties to use the trademark under specific conditions and for defined purposes, while assignments involve the transfer of ownership of the trademark. License agreements and assignments are essential in managing and commercializing trademarks while ensuring proper quality control and brand consistency.

International Trademark Protection: Businesses operating in multiple jurisdictions can seek trademark protection internationally through treaties and agreements such as the Madrid Protocol and the Paris Convention. These agreements provide a streamlined process for filing and managing international trademark registrations, simplifying the protection of trademarks across different countries.

Understanding the Law of Trademarks is crucial for businesses to protect their brands, establish brand recognition, and prevent unauthorized use or infringement. It is recommended to consult with legal professionals specialized in trademark law to navigate the complexities of trademark registration, enforcement, and licensing, ensuring compliance with applicable laws and maximizing the value of trademarks in business strategies.